# Attention-Deficit/Hyperactivity Disorder
## in Children and Adults

## About the Authors

**Annette U. Rickel, PhD,** is Professor of Psychology at Cornell University Medical College in New York City and is in clinical practice. She received her Doctorate from the University of Michigan and most recently was a Professor of Psychiatry at Georgetown University Medical Center. Dr. Rickel is a fellow and past President of the American Psychological Association's Society for Community Research and Action, and was a fellow of the American Council on Education. She was a Senior Congressional Science Fellow in the U.S. Senate from 1992–1994, and served on President Clinton's Task Force for National Health Care Reform. Dr. Rickel has received several research awards from institutions such as the National Institute of Mental Health, as well as the MacArthur and Kellogg Foundations. She has been a Consulting Editor for the American Journal of Community Psychology, the Journal of Community Psychology, and the Journal of Primary Prevention, and serves on the Board of Directors of many non-profit organizations. Dr. Rickel has authored or coauthored six books, numerous research articles, and chapters that deal with early intervention programs for individuals at high risk for psychopathology.

**Ronald T. Brown, PhD,** ABPP is Professor of Public Health, Psychology and Pediatrics and is Dean of the College of Health Professions at Temple University. Dr. Brown is a diplomate in Clinical Health Psychology of the American Board of Professional Psychology, and is a fellow of the American Psychological Association, the American Psychological Society, the Society of Behavioral Medicine, and the National Academy of Neuropsychology. Dr. Brown has been the recipient of numerous grant awards from the National Institutes of Health, the Centers for Disease Control and Prevention, the Department of Defense and the Office of Special Education and Rehabilitation Services. Dr. Brown currently is the Editor of the Journal of Pediatric Psychology and serves of the Behavioral Medicine and Intervention Outcomes of the Center for Scientific Review of the National Institutes of Health. He has published over 200 articles, chapters, and books related to childhood psychopathology and health psychology. He also has served on the editorial boards of 11 journals related to child and adolescent psychopathology. Dr. Brown also serves as a liaison to the American Academy of Pediatric subcommittee on the assessment and practice guidelines for attention-deficit/hyperactivity disorder. Dr. Brown also serves as Chair of the Board of Scientific Affairs of the American Psychological Association.

## Advances in Psychotherapy – Evidence-Based Practice

**Danny Wedding;** PhD, MPH, Prof., St. Louis, MO
(Series Editor)
**Larry Beutler;** PhD, Prof., Palo Alto, CA
**Kenneth E. Freedland;** PhD, Prof., St. Louis, MO
**Linda C. Sobell;** PhD, ABPP, Prof., Ft. Lauderdale, FL
**David A. Wolfe;** PhD, Prof., Toronto
(Associate Editors)

The basic objective of this new series is to provide therapists with practical, evidence-based treatment guidance for the most common disorders seen in clinical practice – and to do so in a "reader-friendly" manner. Each book in the series is both a compact "how-to-do" reference on a particular disorder for use by professional clinicians in their daily work, as well as an ideal educational resource for students and for practice-oriented continuing education.

The most important feature of the books is that they are practical and "reader-friendly": All are structured similarly and all provide a compact and easy-to-follow guide to all aspects that are relevant in real-life practice. Tables, boxed clinical "pearls", marginal notes, and summary boxes assist orientation, while checklists provide tools for use in daily practice.

# Attention-Deficit/ Hyperactivity Disorder
## in Children and Adults

**Annette U. Rickel**
Cornell University Medical College, New York City, NY

**Ronald T. Brown**
College of Health Professions, Temple University, Philadelphia, PA

**Library of Congress Cataloging in Publication**

is available via the Library of Congress Marc Database under the
LC Control Number 2006937671

**Library and Archives Canada Cataloguing in Publication**

Rickel, Annette U.
        Attention-deficit/hyperactivity disorder in children and adults / Annette U.
Rickel, Ronald T. Brown.

(Advances in psychotherapy--evidence-based practice)
Includes bibliographical references.
ISBN 978-0-88937-322-8

1. Attention-deficit hyperactivity disorder.  I. Brown, Ronald T.  II. Title.
III. Series.

RJ506.H9R532 2007              616.85'89              C2006-906262-5

Cover illustration by Klaus Gehrmann

PUBLISHING OFFICES
USA:            Hogrefe & Huber Publishers, 875 Massachusetts Avenue, 7th Floor,
                Cambridge, MA 02139
                Phone (866) 823-4726, Fax (617) 354-6875; E-mail info@hhpub.com
EUROPE:         Hogrefe & Huber Publishers, Rohnsweg 25, 37085 Göttingen, Germany
                Phone +49 551 49609-0, Fax +49 551 49609-88, E-mail hh@hhpub.com

SALES & DISTRIBUTION
USA:            Hogrefe & Huber Publishers, Customer Services Department,
                30 Amberwood Parkway, Ashland, OH 44805
                Phone (800) 228-3749, Fax (419) 281-6883, E-mail custserv@hhpub.com
EUROPE:         Hogrefe & Huber Publishers, Rohnsweg 25, 37085 Göttingen, Germany
                Phone +49 551 49609-0, Fax +49 551 49609-88, E-mail hh@hhpub.com

OTHER OFFICES
CANADA:         Hogrefe & Huber Publishers, 1543 Bayview Avenue, Toronto, Ontario M4G 3B5
SWITZERLAND: Hogrefe & Huber Publishers, Länggass-Strasse 76, CH-3000 Bern 9

Hogrefe & Huber Publishers
Incorporated and registered in the State of Washington, USA, and in Göttingen, Lower Saxony,
Germany

Printed and bound in the USA
ISBN 978-0-88937-322-8

# Preface

Attention-Deficit/Hyperactivity Disorder (ADHD) is a common disorder that affects as many as 7% of children and accounts for 30–40% of all referrals made to child guidance clinics. Yet it is one of the most difficult disorders to define. As has been shown in recent years, ADHD continues into adulthood for many individuals, and can have serious consequences for academic, emotional, social, and occupational functioning. When properly identified and diagnosed, however, there are many interventions for the disorder that have established benefits.

Substantial knowledge has been gained on the neurobiology, heritability, comorbidity, pharmacological and psychotherapeutic treatment of children, adolescents, and adults with ADHD. Readers will gain an understanding of recent advances in the etiology and symptom presentations of ADHD in children and adults. The volume will also educate practitioners on topics such as the specific assessment procedures clinicians need to interpret for a diagnosis of ADHD as well as the use of stimulant medications and the possible side effects associated with pharmacological interventions. The volume further elaborates on common co-occurring conditions such as learning disabilities, substance abuse, depressive, and anxiety disorders. In addition, it will focus on effective psychotherapies, including individual behavioral techniques, peer and school-based interventions, and career related advocacy and guidance with adults. Finally, the federal mandates that ensure the rights of individuals with ADHD are presented and relevant legal issues are explored.

The volume is both a compact "how to" reference, for use by professional clinicians in their daily work, and an ideal educational resource for practice-oriented students. The most important feature of this volume is that it is practical and "reader friendly." It has a similar structure to others in the series, and is a compact and easy to follow guide covering all aspects of practice that are relevant in real life in the assessment and management of ADHD across the life span. Tables, relevant case studies, and marginal notes assist orientation, while suggestions for further reading, support groups, and educational organizations are provided for individuals and professionals.

## Acknowledgments

We are indebted to the following individuals who have supported and assisted us in this endeavor. The work of Rachael Goldsmith, PhD, was invaluable and significant in bringing this volume to completion. In addition, the assistance provided by Victor Rubino, Esq., is also very much appreciated.

Annette U. Rickel, PhD, New York, NY
Ronald T. Brown, PhD, Philadelphia, PA

# Table of Contents

# 1

# Description of Attention-Deficit/ Hyperactivity Disorder

## 1.1   Terminology

Attention-deficit/hyperactivity disorder (ADHD) is a neurodevelopmental disorder characterized by developmentally inappropriate levels of inattention, impulsivity, and/or overactivity that result in chronic functional impairments across settings (American Psychiatric Association, 2000). ADHD also is accompanied by cognitive and behavioral manifestations that usually emerge during the childhood years. The Diagnostic and Statistical Manual for Mental Disorders, Fourth Edition, Text Revision (DSM-IV-TR; American Psychiatric Association, 2000) lists ADHD under the following codes:

314.01  Attention-Deficit/Hyperactivity Disorder, Combined Type

314.00  Attention-Deficit/Hyperactivity Disorder, Predominantly Inattentive Type

314.01  Attention-Deficit/Hyperactivity Disorder, Predominantly Hyperactive-Impulsive Type

The International Classification of Diseases, 10th edition, (ICD-10; World Health Organization, 1992) lists ADHD under code F90 "Hyperkinetic Disorders" and F90.0 under "Disturbance of Activity and Attention". ADHD has had a checkered history where a great deal of myth and misconception has guided both the diagnosis and the management of the disorder. The disorder has been known earlier by other names such as "brain damaged syndrome," "minimal brain dysfunction," "hyperkinetic impulsive disorder," and "attention deficit disorder". The changes in terminology have generally reflected our increasing understanding pertaining to the etiology, identification, and appropriate management of the disorder in more recent years.

## 1.2   Definition

According to the **DSM-IV-TR**, specific diagnostic criteria for ADHD include developmentally inappropriate levels of inattention, impulsivity, and/or overactivity as follows:

I. Either A or B

A. Six or more of the following symptoms of inattention have been present for at least six months to a point that is disruptive and inappropriate for the developmental level:

Inattention:
1. Often does not give close attention to details or makes careless mistakes in schoolwork, work, or other activities
2. Often has trouble keeping attention on tasks or play activities
3. Often does not seem to listen when spoken to directly
4. Often does not follow instructions and fails to finish schoolwork, chores, or duties in the workplace (not due to oppositional behavior or failure to understand instructions)
5. Often has trouble organizing activities
6. Often avoids, dislikes, or doesn't want to do things that take a lot of mental effort for a long period of time (such as schoolwork or homework)
7. Often loses things needed for tasks and activities (e.g., toys, school assignments, pencils, books, or tools)
8. Is often easily distracted
9. Is often forgetful in daily activities

B. Six or more of the following symptoms of hyperactivity-impulsivity have been present for at least six months to an extent that is disruptive and inappropriate for the developmental level:

Hyperactivity:
1. Often fidgets with hands or feet or squirms in seat
2. Often gets up from seat when remaining in seat is required
3. Often runs about or climbs when and where it is not appropriate (adolescents or adults may feel very restless)
4. Often has trouble playing or enjoying leisure activities quietly
5. Is often "on the go" or often acts as if "driven by a motor"
6. Often talks excessively

Impulsivity:
1. Often blurts out answers before questions have been finished
2. Often has trouble waiting one's turn
3. Often interrupts or intrudes on others (e.g., butts into conversations or games)

II. Some symptoms that cause impairment were present before age seven years.

III. Some impairment from the symptoms is present in two or more settings (e.g., at school/work and at home).

IV. There must be clear evidence of significant impairment in social, school, or work functioning.

V. The symptoms do not happen only during the course of a pervasive developmental disorder, schizophrenia, or psychotic disorder. The symptoms are not more appropriately accounted for by another mental disorder (e.g., mood disorder, anxiety disorder, disseminative disorder, or a personality disorder).

Based on these criteria, three types of ADHD are identified:
1. ADHD, Combined Type: if both criteria 1A and 1B are met for the past six months
2. ADHD, Predominantly Inattentive Type: if criterion 1A is met but criterion 1B is not met for the past six months
3. ADHD, Predominantly Hyperactive-Impulsive Type: if Criterion 1B is met but Criterion 1A is not met for the past six months

According to the **ICD-10**, the definition is as follows:
F90. Hyperkinetic disorders: A group of disorders characterized by an early onset (usually in the first five years of life), lack of persistence in activities that require cognitive involvement, and a tendency to move from one activity to another without completing any one, together with disorganized, ill-regulated, and excessive activity. Several other associated abnormalities may be present. Hyperkinetic children often are reckless and impulsive, prone to accidents, and find themselves in disciplinary trouble because of unthinking breaches of rules, rather than deliberate defiance. Their relationships with adults are often socially dissonant, with a lack of normal caution and reserve. They are unpopular with other children and may become isolated. Impairment of cognitive functions is common, and specific delays in motor and language development are disproportionately frequent. Secondary complications include dissocial behavior and low self-esteem (World Health Organization, 1992).

Excludes:    Anxiety disorders
             Mood [affective] disorders
             Pervasive developmental disorders
             Schizophrenia
F90.0 Disturbance of activity and attention:
Attention deficit:
     Disorder with hyperactivity
     Hyperactivity disorder
     Syndrome with hyperactivity
This definition **excludes** hyperkinetic disorder associated with conduct disorder.

One major problem with current psychiatric nomenclature is that the disorder as currently conceptualized is significantly symptom-driven. In making a diagnosis, particular weight is given to symptoms such as inattention and impulsivity rather than the functional impairments associated with the disorder which may be especially impairing in different settings, such as home, school, or with peers.

## 1.3    Epidemiology

### 1.3.1    Prevalence

It is estimated that ADHD is prevalent in about 3% to 7.5% of the school age population (depending on which source is reported), or from 1.4 to almost 3 million of school age children in any given year (Barkley, 2006). In general, approximately 5% of the school-aged population in the United States meets the criteria for this disorder (American Psychiatric Association, 2000). Prevalence of the disorder frequently varies according to informant (caregiver, teacher). However, studies of the incidence of ADHD vary greatly depending on the strictness of the criteria. In one of the more carefully conducted studies at the Mayo Clinic in Rochester, Minnesota, which included a clinical diagnosis and supporting documentation from medical and school records, St. Sauver, Barbaresi, Katusic, Colligan, Weaver, and Jacobsen. (2004) concluded that

**3–5% of school age children have ADHD**

7.5% of school-age children in the district had ADHD. There are some experts who have argued that the incidence of the disorder is more prevalent than incidence data may suggest (Barkley, 2006), with a number of children and adolescents not receiving appropriate management for this disorder.

## 1.3.2   Gender

**ADHD is more frequent in males than females**

The disorder occurs more frequently in males than in females, with ratios ranging from 2:1 to 6:1 (Biederman, Lopez, Boellner, & Chandler, 2002). Although more common in boys than girls, the actual impact of ADHD can be more severe in girls. Some experts have posited that girls do not exhibit the same overt conduct problems or disruptive behaviors as do their male counter parts. This, in part, may account for fewer referrals of females for mental health services simply because their behavioral problems are not a disturbance to others. In recent years, there has been a significant increase in the documented prevalence of ADHD among females, which some experts have attributed to more careful identification of the specific subtypes of the disorder, especially the primarily inattentive subtype (Barkley, 2006).

## 1.3.3   Age

ADHD typically emerges early in life and is a chronic disorder that places children and adolescents at higher than average risk for academic, behavioral, and social difficulties. While ADHD is usually evident before the age of seven, it can persist into adolescence and adulthood. There is some emerging research to suggest that early symptoms of the disorder that may be prevalent during preschool, are especially predictive of a more severe presentation later in childhood, as well as a more difficult course of the disorder (Campbell, 1990). Thus, treatment should begin as soon as possible, address multiple areas of functioning, and be implemented across settings and over long periods of time.

ADHD symptoms manifest differently in adults than in children. Since the disorder was initially conceptualized as a disorder of childhood, the symptom descriptions reflect manifestations of the disorder in children. The DSM-IV formulation constitutes an improvement over the previous criteria, but the descriptions still read as though they are primarily geared towards children (Weiss et al., 1999). Although about 60% of children with ADHD continue to have the disorder as adults (Elliott, 2002), and about 2–10% of adults qualify for the disorder under current criteria, there exists at times a misperception among the public and even among some health care professionals that ADHD is not a real phenomenon among adults (Weiss et al., 1999). For many individuals, ADHD symptoms shift throughout the lifespan. When individuals develop from childhood into adolescence and later into adulthood, hyperactive symptoms may diminish, whereas difficulties with distractibility and inattention persist (Nadeau, 2005).

## 1.3.4    Problems in Adulthood

The same children who experience restlessness as children may find that that they need to incorporate a great deal of activity into their jobs and lives (Adler, 2004). They may become agitated if they are required to work in situations that are too sedentary or monotonous. For many individuals with ADHD, restlessness transitions from psychomotor agitation to an increase in goal-directed activities. At times, restlessness among adults with ADHD can have positive outcomes, as such individuals may be able to work on several jobs or projects simultaneously, and often bring energy to their environments (Weiss et al., 1999).

**ADHD is usually evident before the age of 7**

Many adults with ADHD experience challenges in their workplaces. Symptoms of inattention, which may not have been the most disabling aspect of the disorder for individuals when they were children, can present serious difficulties for adults with ADHD at work. They may struggle to meet deadlines, organize materials, prioritize tasks, and manage their time. Weiss et al. (1999) identify time management and procrastination as ADHD patients' greatest obstacles. These issues may relate to initiating, completing, and switching tasks. These impairments can have serious consequences in terms of educational attainment and career advancement. High-functioning adults with ADHD are often able to progress through their initial schooling because of their intelligence, but as their environments become more demanding, the disorder can limit their achievement. Emotional effects can include difficulties with self-regulation and feelings of being overwhelmed or out of control (Nadeau, 2005).

Just as inattention may present a more serious difficulty for adults with ADHD than for children with the disorder, symptoms of impulsivity can also have serious consequences. Adults with ADHD may find themselves ending jobs or relationships suddenly and against their better interests. They may also make unfortunate financial decisions, including impulsive shopping. These experiences can result in self-blame and exacerbate the problems with self-esteem that are experienced by many individuals with ADHD.

ADHD also affects adults' personal relationships. The disorder can influence individuals' parenting styles and their intimate relationships. Symptoms of restlessness can impact friendships and romantic relationships, as individuals with ADHD may be less eager to engage in relaxing activities than their friends or partners. Adults with ADHD may often be late or miss appointments or social events. They often have limited abilities to manage frustration; they often become angry easily, but may express their anger inappropriately.

There are several other possible manifestations of ADHD among adults. Adults with ADHD are more likely to have automobile accidents than adults without the disorder (Barkley, Murphy, & Kwasnik, 1996). These accidents are also more serious than accidents among those without ADHD. Besides the effects of ADHD symptoms on adult relationships and work performance, the symptoms can result in difficulties paying bills, completing taxes, or answering messages or correspondence (Weiss et al., 1999). Another common issue is mood lability, which can affect perceptions of social interactions and self-esteem.

Weiss et al. (1999) describe features of ADHD in adults that are often central to their patients' experience, but do not currently appear among the criteria listed in the DSM. They identify procrastination, a persistent sense of failure, poor time management, and a tendency to take on more tasks than can be completed as core presenting symptoms of adults with ADHD. Weiss et al. offer the following descriptions listed in Table 1 of the ways adults with ADHD may present symptoms of the disorder.

**Table 1**
**Adult Presentations of ADHD Symptoms**

| DSM-IV Criteria for Inattentive Subtype | Adult Presentation |
| --- | --- |
| 1. Often fails to give close attention to details or makes careless mistakes in schoolwork, work, or other activities. | Adults with ADHD may experience trouble remembering where they have put things. This may lead to problems at work. They may struggle with tasks that require attention to detail or that are tedious, such as income tax preparation. |
| 2. Often has difficulty sustaining attention in tasks or play activities. | Adults with ADHD may fail to complete tasks, such as cleaning a room, without interrupting the task to begin a new one. They may be unable to sustain their attention long enough to read a book, write letters, pay bills, or keep accounts. |
| 3. Often does not seem to listen when spoken to directly. | Adults with ADHD may be told that they are inadequate listeners, that they do not seem to understand what was said, or that it is hard to obtain their attention. They may often appear "tuned out." |
| 4. Often does not follow through on instructions and fails to finish schoolwork, chores, or duties in the workplace. | Adults with ADHD can experience challenges in following others' instructions, and may struggle to read or follow directions in manuals. They also may fail to follow through on the commitments they make. |
| 5. Often has difficulty organizing tasks or activities. | Adults with ADHD may exhibit chronic lateness, and often miss deadlines and appointments. They may delegate some tasks to others, such as a spouse or secretary, who are more capable in this domain. |
| 6. Often avoids, dislikes, or is reluctant to engage in tasks that require sustained mental effort (such as schoolwork or homework). | Adults with ADHD often put off responding to mail, answering letters, organizing papers, paying taxes or bills, or establishing appropriate insurance or a will. They often report difficulties with procrastination. |

**Table 1** (continued)

| | | |
|---|---|---|
| 7. | Often loses things necessary for tasks or activities (e.g., toys, school assignments, pencils, books, or tools). | Adults with ADHD may lose their keys or wallets easily. They may forget where they parked their cars. Parents may have difficulty remembering their children's schedules and their obligations for transportation or appointments. |
| 8. | Is often easily distracted by extraneous stimuli. | Adults with ADHD can feel distracted or overwhelmed by stimuli in their environment. Sometimes parents may respond to the normal behavior of their children by feeling overwhelmed. |
| 9. | Is often forgetful in daily activities. | Adults with ADHD may report problems with memory and planning. |

| DSM-IV Criteria for Hyperactivity | Adult Presentations |
|---|---|

| | | |
|---|---|---|
| 1. | Often fidgets with hands or feet or squirms in seat. | Adults with ADHD can exhibit observable fidgeting, including shaking their knees, tapping their hands or feet, changing their positions, or picking their fingers. |
| 2. | Often leaves seat in classroom or in other situations in which remaining seated is expected. | Adults with ADHD may have trouble sitting still during conversations, or have difficulties with restlessness in situations where they must wait. |
| 3. | Often runs about or climbs excessively in situations in which it is inappropriate (may be limited to subjective feelings or restlessness in adolescents or adults). | Adults with ADHD sometimes report feelings of needing to be constantly "on the go" or requiring stimulating activities. Patients may pace or fidget during interviews. |
| 4. | Often has difficulty playing or engaging in leisure activities quietly. | Adults with ADHD are often reluctant to stay at home or to partake in quiet activities. Many individuals report being workaholics. In this case, an assessment should evaluate the details of the patient's needs for constant work. |
| 5. | Is often "on the go" or often acts as if "driven by a motor." | Family members, friends, and intimate partners may report that they experience fatigue after being around adults with ADHD. They may have trouble meeting the pace and expectations of adults with ADHD. |
| 6. | Often talks excessively. | For adults with ADHD, constant verbiage may make conversational exchanges difficult, and can prevent others around them from feeling heard or understood. |

**Table 1** (continued)

| DSM-IV Criteria for Impulsivity | Adult Presentations |
|---|---|
| 7. Often blurts out answers before questions have been completed. | Health professionals may observe this feature in adults with ADHD. Some individuals may experience this symptom as related to their perceptions that other people are talking too slowly and that it is difficult to wait for them to finish speaking. |
| 8. Often has difficulty awaiting turn. | Adults with ADHD can experience difficulties waiting for children to finish tasks at a developmentally appropriate pace, and can have trouble waiting in line. |
| 9. Often interrupts or intrudes on others (e.g., butts into conversations or games). | Adults with ADHD may interrupt frequently in social or work situations, which can result in feelings of social ineptness. |

(Adapted from Weiss et al., 1999)

### 1.3.5    Ethnicity

The prevalence of ADHD is similar across ethnic groups

ADHD occurs across nationalities and cultures at similar rates. Cross-cultural research demonstrates similar rates of prevalence and heritability of ADHD. For instance, Rohde, Szobot, Polanczyk, Schmitz, Martins, and Tramontina (2005) performed a meta-analysis of data pertaining to diagnostic patterns of ADHD in Brazil, and notes patterns of familial continuity and comorbidity rates similar to those observed in other developed countries. Environmental factors such as classroom size and cultural backgrounds may, however, influence teachers' appraisals of those students who are identified as having symptoms associated with ADHD (Havey, Olson, McCormick, & Cates, 2005). These perceptions also may influence the course of the disorder. Unfortunately, there are few studies looking at ADHD across cultures and ethnic groups. Clearly, this is an important issue destined for future investigation.

There are no studies concerning ethnic distribution of this disorder, but there is some evidence that people of color have poorer access to appropriate services for the disorder and hence receive less treatment and are less likely to be referred for treatment than whites. Ethnicity may influence the way parents, teachers, and practitioners perceive ADHD symptoms, and therefore adversely impact the likelihood of whether ADHD will be identified and appropriately treated.

## 1.4    Course and Prognosis

ADHD usually manifests itself in childhood. If left untreated it can lead to academic failure and difficulties in relating to peers. The disorder is frequently associated with a number of other comorbid psychiatric disorders that include externalizing or disruptive behaviors (e.g., oppositional defiant disorder, conduct disorder) as well as internalizing disorders (e.g., anxiety, depression). There is some evidence that when ADHD is comorbid with other disorders, it may have a different course or even a more guarded prognosis (Lahey, McBurnett, & Loeber, 2000). An ADHD child finds it difficult to plan ahead and pick up on social cues. In short, if left untreated ADHD does not "go away" and can have substantial adverse consequences for the quality of the person's life.

**ADHD is often comorbid with other psychiatric disorders**

Because ADHD is a chronic disorder and places children and adolescents at high risk for a number of functional impairments, treatment must begin early in life, address multiple domains of functioning, and be implemented across multiple settings and over long periods of time. Despite some of the most intensive treatment efforts for the disorder, most children with ADHD (over 80%) still continue to evidence symptoms of the disorder in adolescence (Tannock & Brown, 2000) and even adulthood (Barkley, Murphy, O'Connell, & Connor, 2005), although the disorder may be more "controlled" through lifestyle choices.

## 1.5     Differential Diagnosis

There are several psychiatric and physical disorders that share some of the signs and symptoms of ADHD that need to be considered by the practitioner. The ICD-10 highlights the importance of a single diagnostic category that best expresses the psychological profile of an individual, whereas practitioners using the DSM-IV often diagnose patients with multiple disorders (Newcorn & Halperin, 2000), recognizing that there are several comorbid disorders that occur with ADHD.

Some symptoms of ADHD, such as difficulties with concentration, may overlap with other internalizing behaviors such as depression, anxiety, and posttraumatic stress disorder (PTSD), as illustrated in Table 2. Though many cases of ADHD remain untreated or incorrectly identified, other individuals may believe they suffer from ADHD, when in fact they are experiencing symptoms associated with other disorders including anxiety or depression.

**ADHD symptoms may overlap with those of depression, anxiety, and posttraumatic stress disorder**

Although some individuals may feel stigmatized by the possibility of an ADHD diagnosis, such stigma is qualitatively different from the feelings others experience from clinical labels of anxiety or depression. For this reason, some clients may hope for an ADHD diagnosis. In other cases, individuals may seek an ADHD diagnosis in order to obtain more favorable academic conditions, such as more time for tests. Though academic accommodations are often appropriate for individuals with ADHD, clinicians should be aware that some individuals without the disorder also may feign symptoms in order to obtain such accommodations. A major differential feature between ADHD and other psychiatric disorders is the constitutional predisposition toward problems with attention, impulsivity and for some overactivity as well as the long course of the disorder.

ADHD (except for the primarily inattentive group), oppositional defiance disorder (ODD), conduct disorder (CD) share some common core character-

ADHD, ODD, and
CD share common
characteristics, but
with increasing anti-
social behavior
istics such as impulsive behavior, interrupting others, difficulty waiting one's turn, etc., but there exist symptoms of increasingly severe antisocial behavior as we move from ADHD to ODD to CD. There also is some evidence that ADHD may synergize ODD and CD (Newcorn & Halperin, 2000)

Clinicians should assess for ADHD when a child presents with ODD or CD. What makes diagnosis especially difficult is that there can be isolated instances of the more severe symptoms of ODD and CD in an ADHD child. Thus, children may frequently have comorbid ADHD and CD and this co-morbid presentation may actually appear to be more severe than ADHD than when it presents without comorbidity. There is evidence that CD may actually exacerbate or synergize symptoms of ADHD, and hence it is necessary to manage both disorders carefully. There are many therapies that have been used successfully to treat both disorders, including behavior management and family systems therapy, and these therapies are appropriate for all of the disorders discussed in this section. Data even suggest that careful management of the symptoms for ADHD may assist in the treatments for other comorbid disorders.

Specific learning disabilities (LD), whether dyslexia, spelling, writing, or math disorders, share a number of the outward ADHD symptoms such as difficulty following instructions or shifting from one uncompleted task to another but may be more bound up with the LD as the core issue to be resolved. Thus, coping with dyslexia may make a child more attentive and more able to follow instructions. Frequently, many children who receive a diagnosis of ADHD also have comorbidity of learning disabilities. In general, the management of the two disorders differs, whereby the specific management of a learning disability involves various cognitive and special educational or remedial approaches.

**Table 2**
**Overlapping symptoms between ADHD and other psychiatric disorders**

| ADHD symptom or associated feature | Depres-sion | Mania | PTSD | GAD | Substance use disorders |
|---|---|---|---|---|---|
| Difficulty sustaining attention | X | | X | X | X |
| Easily distracted | | X | | | |
| Fidgets | X | | | X | |
| Constantly "on the go" | X | X | | X | X |
| Often talks excessively | | X | | | |
| Mood lability | | X | | | X |
| Low self-esteem | X | | | | |
| Temper outbursts | | X | | | X |
| Demoralization | X | | | | |
| Dysphoria | X | | | | X (during withdrawal) |

It is important for the practitioner to look for the key differential characteristics of each of the above disorders.

Comorbid disorders are important to diagnose as they may require other treatment

## 1.6     Comorbidities in ADHD Patients

Comorbid disorders that may accompany ADHD may include CD (20–40% of ADHD children), ODD (33–50% of ADHD children), or LD (involving 20–30% of ADHD children). In addition, the anxiety disorders that include overanxious disorder, separation anxiety disorder, generalized anxiety disorder or the various mood disorders such as major depressive disorder can also co-occur with ADHD. Comorbid psychiatric disorders that occur with ADHD are important to recognize and diagnose as these comorbid disorders dictate other treatment interventions that may be necessary, or they could possibly suggest specific treatment management for ADHD (Biederman, Faraone, & Lapey, 1992).

Approximately 20–25% of children who present with ADHD have specific learning disorders. Tannock and Brown (2000) observe that some children with ADHD and LD appear to be fidgety and inattentive, and may have difficulty following complex conversations. Tannock and Brown note that academic performance for these children often seems slow and inaccurate in children with comorbid ADHD and LD, whereas performance for ADHD alone is rapid and inaccurate. There is some research to suggest that there are various subtypes of children with ADHD. For example, these may include a group of "fast inaccurates" as well "slow inaccurates" that represent different clusters of ADHD children without and with comorbid learning disabilities.

In addition to the disorders discussed in the previous section – ODD, CD and LD – some children with ADHD often have comorbid disorders associated with anxiety and depression. The appropriate management of either ADHD or the anxiety and depression can have a positive effect on the child's functional outcomes (e.g., academic performance, peer socialization).

Bipolar disorder is a psychiatric disorder that has been increasingly recognized in children and adolescents and can often be comorbid in children and adolescents with ADHD. The differential diagnosis between bipolar disorder and ADHD can be especially difficult because there are specific symptoms that can be present in both disorders that include a high level of energy and reduced need for sleep. One of the key differentiators is the elated mood and grandiosity of the bipolar child that is not always present and sometimes dissipates for several weeks or even months. For those children and adolescents with ADHD, symptoms are typically pervasive and ever present over time.

About one in four children who present with ADHD may also be diagnosed with one or more of the anxiety disorders (Tannock & Brown, 2000). In fact, Biederman, Faraone, Spencer, Wilens, Norman, Lapey et al. (1993) found that over half (52%) of adults referred with ADHD met criteria for two or more major anxiety disorders. Tannock and Brown (2000) describe children with co-occurring anxiety disorders and ADHD as "worriers." Unlike children who have ADHD only, children who have both an anxiety disorder and ADHD demonstrate explicit symptoms of anxiety, and they evidence undue concerns about their skills and performance in social situations and in academic settings.

Research has been inconsistent as to how anxiety disorders may affect ADHD and the presence of symptoms associated with ADHD. Children with comorbid anxiety disorders and ADHD are more likely to be experiencing stressful life events than those children with ADHD alone.

There is some evidence from the neuropsychological literature to suggest that children with comorbid ADHD and anxiety disorders are more competent at some neuropsychological tasks associated with attention and concentration (e.g., the Continuous Performance Test), yet also exhibit greater impairments on other tasks (e.g., the Serial Addition Task). However, additional research is necessary to determine the ways comorbidity influences performance on neuropsychological tests.

**Children with comorbid ADHD and anxiety do not benefit from stimulant medication and may show increased side effects**

Tannock and Brown (2000) observe that children presenting with comorbid ADHD and anxiety disorders have low self-esteem that is exacerbated by low levels of social and academic functioning. Again, the identification of these comorbidities is important as there is some evidence that children with comorbid anxiety and ADHD derive fewer cognitive and behavioral benefits from stimulant medications, and report a greater frequency of adverse side effects from the stimulants, than do their peers who are identified as ADHD without comorbidities (Tannock & Brown, 2000).

**Comorbid mood disorders are common in individuals with ADHD**

Clinicians should routinely assess for the possible presence of symptoms associated with depression and anxiety in patients for whom the diagnosis of ADHD has been made. Likewise, the astute diagnostician should be alert for behavioral signs of anxiety in children who present with ADHD. Such symptoms may include, but are not limited to, motor tension, separation anxiety, nervous mannerisms, and speech abnormalities. Although parents and teachers may be the best informants regarding children's observable behaviors and symptoms associated with ADHD, children are often better sources of information regarding symptoms of internalizing behavior (anxiety, depression) (Tannock & Brown, 2000).

Mood disorders are also common in individuals with ADHD. The most common mood difficulty related to ADHD is emotional lability (Weiss et al., 1999). Individuals with ADHD frequently exhibit rapid mood alterations, and often do not demonstrate awareness for the triggers affecting these changes. Because of these rapid changes, individuals with ADHD who also have comorbid depression may endorse depressive symptoms, but report that the depression has not been consistent most of the day for two weeks or more. Another common symptom of children with ADHD who have significant comorbid depressive symptoms is a tendency to inflate the importance of difficult events and the belief that they have little control over the effects of stress. These patients may exhibit irritability, anger, and social dysfunction as a result of their ADHD symptoms.

**Side effects of stimulant medication may be similar to symptoms of depression**

Individuals with ADHD who are being managed with stimulant medication may also have problems associated with the adverse side effects of medication, such as loss of appetite, anxiety, dysthymia, insomnia, physical complaints, and irritability. It is especially noteworthy that of the nine DSM criteria for depression, several of these symptoms overlap with the adverse effects associated with stimulant medication. These symptoms include decreased interest in activities, appetite disturbances, insomnia, psychomotor agitation or retardation, feelings of worthlessness, fatigue, and poor concentration. Because of the overlap between depressive symptoms and the adverse effects of stimulant medication, the course of symptom development may be the most useful way of differentiating between ADHD, treatment with stimulant medication, and the possibility of depression.

In order to support a diagnosis of comorbid ADHD and depression, clinicians need to carefully assess whether individuals experience a consistently depressed affect for two weeks or more. Biederman, Faraone, et al. (1993) found that nearly one-third (31%) of adults they managed for ADHD met full diagnostic criteria for major depressive disorder, and Faraone, Biederman, Mennin, Wozniak, and Spencer (1997) found that about 30% of adults with ADHD report having experienced symptoms consistent with depression during childhood. It is also noteworthy that persons with ADHD and depression may be at increased risk for accidents and suicidal behavior than individuals with only one of these disorders. Hence, the astute practitioner should always be vigilant for the presence for suicidal ideation, gestures, or behaviors.

ADHD may pose an especially salient risk factor for substance abuse disorders, and also may influence the onset and recovery of drug substance and alcohol use. Individuals with ADHD are more likely to use drugs and alcohol, and to use them at earlier ages than those without ADHD. In addition, individuals with ADHD are much more likely to develop a substance use disorder than individuals without ADHD. For example Biederman, Thisted, Greenhill, and Ryan (1995) have noted that there is a 52% lifetime prevalence of substance abuse disorders for those with ADHD, and a 27% without ADHD. Some individuals may use substances to medicate their ADHD symptoms. Research has demonstrated that groups affected by the comorbidity of bipolar disorder or conduct disorder with ADHD have the highest likelihood of abusing some type of alcohol or drug substance and to eventually meet criteria for a substance use disorder (Wilens, Spencer, & Biederman, 2000a). Individuals with ADHD tend to abuse drugs more frequently than they abuse alcohol. In addition, there is an association between nicotine substances and ADHD, and ADHD adolescents being using cigarettes at an earlier age than their typically developing peers. Pomerleau, Downey, Stelson, and Pomerleau (1995) found that adults with ADHD have a risk for nicotine use that is three times greater than the risk for individuals without ADHD. Individuals with ADHD may also consume caffeine and nicotine in greater quantities than individuals who do not have symptoms associated with the disorder.

**Individuals with ADHD are more at risk of developing substance abuse disorders, and likely to start abusing substances earlier than peers**

Children, adolescents, and adults with ADHD also report having greater difficulties with sleep than do their normally developing counterparts. Many individuals with ADHD report consistent problems with falling asleep and remaining alert throughout the day. Parents may notice that children with ADHD have always struggled with falling asleep at night or have encountered difficulties with napping. Individuals with ADHD also may exhibit difficulty awakening, even when they obtain an acceptable amount of sleep during the previous night. This difficulty may manifest itself in terms of being late for school or work. Finally, people with ADHD often have trouble staying alert throughout the day. Many report problems staying awake if they have to sit still for long periods of time or perform routine tasks. Students commonly report falling asleep in lectures, even when they have had an appropriate amount of sleep. Clinicians may misdiagnose a sleep disorder as ADHD, or may even

**Sleep routines may be disrupted in individuals with ADHD**

miss sleep disorders among individuals diagnosed as ADHD. All ADHD assessments should include questions regarding sleep routines, daytime sleepiness, patterns and persistence of sleep difficulties as well as issues pertaining to sleep hygiene.

## 1.7     Diagnostic Procedures and Documentation

**As ADHD is such an encompassing disorder, a team of health care professionals is often used for diagnosis and treatment**

A professional with specific training in ADHD as well as the identification of other psychiatric disorders should make the diagnosis. This might include clinical or school psychologists, child psychiatrists, developmental/behavioral pediatricians, or behavioral neurologists. Because the disorder is so encompassing and impacts a number of domains, such as the home setting and the academic setting, many professionals use a team approach for either diagnosis or management, or frequently both.

The first step is for the professional to accumulate information that will rule out other possible causes of ADHD symptoms that might include symptoms of anxiety or depression; a situational stressor such as the death of a parent or grandparent or parental divorce, learning disability resulting in underachievement; and medical disorders that may affect central nervous system dysfunction such as temporal lobe seizures.

As an illustration, Tannock and Brown (2000) recommend the following steps when assessing the possibility of concurrent ADHD and LD:

1. Attain the child's familial and developmental history for correlates and risks of a learning disorder;
2. Collect teacher and academic ratings of academic progress among multiple academic subject areas;
3. Assess for learning disorders through recommended methods that might include neuropsychological or traditional psychoeducational assessment;
4. Examine comorbid diagnoses that also might include depression, anxiety, or low self-esteem.

Tannock and Brown (2000) also argue that clinicians should routinely assess for multiple types of learning disorders in ADHD patients.

A complete evaluation for ADHD should include a personal and family history obtained through interviews and observations of the individual, as well as school and medical records and psychological test results. Possible alternative or comorbid diagnoses should also be considered. School and medical records should be reviewed, as there may be indications of hearing or vision problems as well as behavioral difficulties. After meeting with the individual, all information gathered can be compared to the symptoms and diagnostic criteria listed in DSM-IV-TR.

It is also very important to determine whether the classroom, work, or home environments are stressful or chaotic and if possible the individual should be observed in these settings. Such information may provide data with regard to possible stressors that may be exacerbating symptoms and may have important treatment implications. In addition, teachers and caregivers need to rate their observations of the individual's behavior on standardized behavior rating scales in order to assess how the child compares to other children of the same chronological age.

A preponderance of research suggests that neuropsychological tests frequently do not identify ADHD or predict response to treatments for ADHD such as stimulant medication (for a review, see Brown & Daly, in press). However, performance on neuropsychological tests may comprise an important component of diagnosis for other comorbidities such as learning disabilities, and in many circumstances may help clinicians identify specific learning disabilities and the need for special education placement. Frequently, such neuropsychological measures are important for monitoring treatment response, especially response to stimulant drug therapy. Neuropsychological tests that measure attention include the Gordon Diagnostic System (Gordon, 1986), Tests of Variables of Attention (TOVA; Greenberg & Waldman, 1993), and the Conners' Continuous Performance Test (Conners, 1985). Assessments often include tests of verbal working memory, such as the Digit Span Test (e.g., Wechsler, 1997a), the California Verbal Learning Test (Delis, Kramer, Kaplan, & Ober, 1987), the Sentence Repetition Tests (Lezak, 1995), the Children's Memory Scale (Cohen, 1997), the Babcock Story Recall (Babcock, 1930), and the Test of Adolescent Language (Hammill, Brown, Larsen, & Wiederhold, 1994). Other important tests that measure mental flexibility and working memory include the Wisconsin Card Sorting Test (Berg, 1948), the Stroop Color-Word Interference Test (Golden, 1978), the Rey-Osterreith Complex Figure (Osterreith, 1944), and the Paced Auditory Serial Addition Test (Gronwall, 1977). Some of these psychological tests are discussed in greater detail in Chapter 3.

Tests of intelligence and achievement should be given where there is an indication that a learning disability may be involved. Again, it is important to underscore that psychological tests are neither sensitive nor specific in identifying ADHD; rather they are useful in the identification of other comorbidities such as developmental deficits including specific learning disabilities or mental retardation and possibly identifying ADHD symptoms of inattention. The use of a systematic approach in gathering data across all sources from multiple informants is imperative in accurately diagnosing ADHD.

**Tests of intelligence and achievement may help in identifying a comorbid learning disorder**

**Summary**

ADHD is a disorder that affects cognition and behavior, and is characterized by difficulties with inattention and/or hyperactivity. It is often comorbid with other psychological conditions, including affective disorders, anxiety disorders, learning disorders, and conduct or oppositional/defiant disorders. ADHD shares some overlapping features with other conditions, including difficulties with concentration and memory. The presentation of ADHD is somewhat different in children than in adults, and adults may have developed coping strategies that mask the disorder. Diagnosing ADHD requires attention to the diagnostic criteria as specified in the DSM-IV. However, since the description was originally created for children, clinicians should be mindful that ADHD symptoms may be expressed somewhat differently in adults.

# 2

# Theories and Models of ADHD

**There are scant data on the etiology of ADHD**

Psychologists have provided extensive theoretical perspectives pertaining to the nature and the course of ADHD. Despite the extensive research on this disorder, there are actually scant data with regard to its etiology. It is challenging to consider all of the phenomena believed to contribute to the development of the disorder, primarily due to the fact that pathways to the ADHD are largely believed to be heterogeneous. For some individuals, the development of the disorder appears to be heritable. For others, external factors or specific environmental factors may contribute to the phenotype of the presenting symptoms of the disorder. The following descriptions suggest that ADHD is likely to develop from a combination of genetic and environmental factors.

**Most children with ADHD continue to experience symptoms into adolescence and adulthood**

Initially, psychologists believed that ADHD was confined to the childhood years and it was common folklore that most children outgrew the disorder. The common belief was that the disorder did not persist into adolescence or adulthood. However, more recent research has indicated that many ADHD individuals continue to experience symptoms, as well as the majority of diagnostic features, well after childhood (e.g., Mannuzza, Klein, Bessler, Malloy, LaPadula, and Addalli, 1993). In fact, all of the longitudinal prospective follow-up studies that initially examined children with ADHD and followed them into adolescence and young adulthood have documented clearly that ADHD does not result in a benign prognosis during adolescence or adulthood. Achenbach, Howell, McConaughy, & Stanger, (1995) have determined that attention problems are more likely to remain present into adulthood than hyperactivity or impulsivity, and that these attentional problems are also more likely to pose functional impairments. Whitman (2000) notes that some adults with ADHD received the diagnosis as children, while others report having had symptoms during childhood, but are diagnosed and treated for the first time as adults. The extended conceptualization of ADHD in adulthood is believed to have similar etiology as it does in childhood. In essence, both children and adults with ADHD are believed to share the same disorder, with the disorder reflecting a continuum from childhood to adulthood. Therefore, the etiological considerations presented below relate to the disorder as present in both children and adults.

## 2.1    Biological Factors in ADHD

### 2.1.1    Genetic Contributions

Current research is being conducted to identify specific genetic contributions to ADHD. Molecular genetic studies and research investigating twins and adopted children suggest that genes predispose individuals to ADHD. Faraone (2004) has hypothesized that the combined effects of multiple genes, yet to be identified, contribute to the ADHD disorder. Genetic relatives of individuals with ADHD are more likely to have the disorder when compared to nongenetic relatives. In addition, genetic relatives of individuals affected by ADHD are more likely to have symptoms of the disorder than individuals from psychiatric samples or the general population (Cook, 2000). Molecular geneticists have identified genes of the dopamine receptor system as candidate genes for the development of ADHD, with a smaller number of studies addressing genetic risk related to norepinephrine receptors (Hudziak, 2000). Barkley (1998b) believes that neurological and genetic factors are the primary determinants of ADHD, but cautions that most research to date has not demonstrated causality.

> **There appears to be a genetic predisposition to ADHD**

Barkley (1998b) has presented evidence demonstrating substantial heritability in ADHD. However, heritability does not necessarily indicate the presence of genetic transmission. Barkley has reviewed a number of studies indicating, for instance, the greater concordance rate among monozygotic than dyzygotic twins. It is important to note that some of these studies may be affected by rater biases. For example, parents may perceive monozygotic twins as more alike, and consequently rate their ADHD symptoms accordingly. Likewise, research indicates parents exaggerate differences between dizygotic twins. Data from several research studies also demonstrate the existence of gender biases, rater biases, and developmental biases that are often conflated with genetic explanations of ADHD (Hudziak, 2000). In addition, the current categorical diagnostic system of the DSM-IV-TR provides only a dichotomous determination of the disorder's presence. Most twin studies of ADHD use a quantitative approach to address symptoms of inattention and hyperactivity rather than employing the categorical approach of the current psychiatric nomenclature employed by the American Psychiatric Association. Researchers have not identified a gene that is associated specifically with ADHD, and do not necessarily agree on a method of heritable transmission. Other endeavors have attempted to use molecular genetics to explain common etiologies for ADHD and comorbid disorders.

While there is not necessarily a clear genotype for the disorder and the specific genetic mechanism of the disorder remains unknown, it is clear that ADHD is a disorder that does occur in families. There is emerging research related to pharmacogenetics whereby some subtypes of children with specific genetic predispositions have been found to respond positively to specific pharmacotherapies and adversely to others. Thus, the interface of genetics and ADHD is a field that is very fertile for future research efforts.

## 2.1.2    Neurological Factors

It is possible to identify neurophysiological differences between individuals with and without ADHD. Electroencephalographic (EEG) findings provide some insight into the neuroanatomical correlates of ADHD (Loo & Barkley, 2005). Taylor (1999) has provided important guidelines for future research that will augment our understanding of the neuroanatomical correlates and predictors of ADHD.

Studies that have used neuropsychological test to evaluate individuals with ADHD have long suggested deficits in frontal lobe functioning related to verbal fluency, perseveration, motor sequencing, planning, and working memory. Other research indicates decreased cerebral blood flow to prefrontal regions and connected pathways (Barkley, 1998b). In addition, researchers have described neurotransmitter correlates of ADHD, and have emphasized abnormalities in dopaminergic functioning. Dopamine does affect attentional processing, and pharmacotherapies that have affinity to specific transmission of dopamine at the synapses have been effective in assuaging ADHD symptoms (Brown, 2000).

**MRI studies support a neurological basis for ADHD**

The most compelling support for a neurological basis for ADHD comes from magnetic resonance imaging (MRI) studies. Specifically, differences have been demonstrated in the brain regions of those children and adolescents with ADHD relative to comparison control groups (Giedd, Blumenthal, Molloy, & Castellanos, 2001; Hynd, Semrud-Clikeman, Lorys, Novey, & Eliopulos, 1990; Hynd, Semrud-Clikeman, Lorys, Novey, Eliopulos, & Lyytinen, 1991; Hynd, Hern, Novey, Eliopulos, Marshall, Gonzalez, & Voeller, 1993; Semrud-Clikeman, Filpek, Biederman, Steingard, Kennedy, Renshaw, & Bekken, 1994; Zametkin & Rapoport, 1986). Specifically, children with ADHD and those with reading disorders were demonstrated to have smaller right hemisphere plana temporale relative to a comparison control group. However, only the children with reading disabilities were found to have a smaller left plana temporale (Hynd et al., 1990). The same research group examined the corpus callosum, a structure in the brain that aids with transfer of information between the hemispheres. Findings from this research revealed that children with ADHD had a smaller corpus callosum relative to the other groups (Hynd et al., 1991), although attempts to replicate this particular investigation actually failed to confirm consistent differences between children with ADHD and comparison controls (Semrud-Clikeman et al., 1994).

Other investigations have revealed smaller anterior right frontal lobe regions, a smaller size of the caudate nucleus, reversed asymmetry of the head of the caudate, and a smaller globus pallidus region in children with ADHD in comparison to their normally developing peers (Castellanos, Giedd, Eckburg, Marsh, Vaituzis, Kaysen, et al., 1994; Castellanos, Giedd, Marsh, Hamburger, Vaitzuzis, Dickstein et al., 1996). More importantly, there are some impressive studies that have shown that the size of specific regions within the brain (e.g., structures in the basal ganglia and the right frontal lobe) is associated with the magnitude of impairment in the area of attention and inhibition (Semrud-Clikeman, Steingard, Filpek, Biederman, Bekken, & Renshaw, 2000), two cognitive processes that have consistently been demonstrated to be impaired among children with ADHD. Of further interest is the finding by Castellanos and associates (1996) who found smaller cerebellar volume in children with ADHD. As Barkley (2006) has pointed out, these data are consistent with the notion that the cerebellum exerts a major role in executive functioning, another area that has consistently differentiated children with ADHD from their typically developing peers.

More recently, advanced technology has allowed for specific functional activity in various brain regions during the administration of psychological testing. These findings are of particular interest as they have demonstrated clearly that relative to their normally developing peers, children with ADHD have impaired patterns of activation during the administration of tasks associated with attention and inhibition (for a review, see Barkley, 2006). While the use of neuroimaging techniques is not part of the standard clinical assessment battery, they are nonetheless important as they allow for the demonstration of the validity of the role of brain abnormalities in the cognitive and behavioral impairments that has been so consistently been demonstrated for children and adolescents with ADHD (Barkley, 2006).

### 2.1.3 Cognitive Determinants

Researchers have noted connections between ADHD and executive function since children with ADHD exhibit deficits in this area (e.g., Geurts, Verte, Oosterlaan, Roeyers, & Sergeant, 2005; Nigg, 2001). Executive function is a term used to describe a spectrum of the brain's control processes that integrate, focus, activate, and prioritize other neurological functions. External demands on executive function increase as humans develop, and become more complex and important as maturity continues. Neurologists have highlighted working memory as a particularly important component of executive function, as it entails maintaining the focus, context, and processing necessities of immediate information (Brown, 2000). Barkley, Grodzinsky, and DuPaul (1992) found that children with ADHD demonstrated impaired performance on the Stroop task (Golden, 1978), an activity that requires both inhibitory control and persistent attention. This spectrum of impairment may represent diverse risk factors and etiologies (Tannock & Brown, 2000).

**Children with ADHD exhibit impaired executive function**

Various theoretical models of ADHD have been proposed over the past several years, including the notion of defective volitional inhibition and moral regulation of behavior (Still, 1902), the theory of deficient attention, inhibition, arousal, and preference for immediate reward (Douglas, 1983), and the conceptualization of ADHD as a deficit in the sensitivity to reinforcement or rule-governed behavior (Barkley, 1989). Barkley (for a review, see Barkley, 2006) has developed a recent model for conceptualizing the many symptoms associated with ADHD that incorporates children's inability to sustain attention and effort in addition to the numerous other symptoms associated with the disorder.

**Individuals with ADHD have difficulties with inhibition and regulation**

Central in Barkley's (2006) model is the notion of behavioral inhibition. According to Barkley, children with ADHD display greater emotional expression in their reaction to events, have less objectivity in the selection of a response to a specific event, evidence less social perspective-taking, since these children do not delay their initial reactions for a sufficient period of time to take the perspective of others and finally, a diminished capacity to induce drive and motivational states in themselves in the service of goal-directed behavior. According to Barkley, those children with ADHD are more dependent on environmental contingencies relative to their peers without the disorder and also have significant problems in the regulation of emotion.

Nonverbal working memory is another impairment couched within Barkley's model. Working memory refers to the capacity of humans to retain a mental representation of specific events in their mind employing visual imagery and private audition. Thus, for those with ADHD, impairments in nonverbal working memory are manifested in forgetting to do things at specific critical points in time, impairments in the ability to organize and execute actions relative to time, and, finally, reduced forethought which thereby leads to a reduction in the creation of anticipatory actions toward future events.

**Privatization of speech is delayed in children with ADHD**

Privatization of speech is an important hallmark of normal development whereby children are eventually able to develop instructive speech that transfers from observable speech to self-directed or reflective speech. Barkley (2006) maintains that for those with ADHD, privatization of speech is delayed, thereby resulting in greater public speech, less verbal reflection prior to engaging in actions, less organized and rule-governed speech, and most importantly an impaired ability to control one's own behavior and in following the rules and instructions that are provided by others.

According to Barkley (2006), children with ADHD experience significant difficulties in behavioral responses to emotion. Thus, individuals with ADHD evidence greater emotional expression in their reactions to events, less objectivity in the selection of a response to an event, diminished social-perspective-taking due to the fact that individuals with ADHD are unable to take the view of others as well as their own needs into account, and finally, a diminished capacity for motivation that diminishes goal-directed behavior.

Another component of Barkley's model is the reconstitution and internalization of play deficit. Specifically, Barkley (2006) has suggested that children with ADHD are limited in their capacity to analyze and synthesize the formation of both verbal and nonverbal responses to events. Thus, ADHD children have a limited capacity to mentally visualize and generate specific options in directing their behavior toward specific goals that will eventually enable them to succeed in specific situations. Barkley has suggested that such limitations are apparent in daily verbal fluency when children with ADHD must assemble parts of speech into specific messages or when they must hold specific visual images in their mind to solve important problems. Finally, Barkley has suggested that deficits in behavioral inhibition have their origins in the brain's motor or output system, which is manifested by impairments in motor coordination and the planning and execution of complex and novel chains of goal directed behavior.

**Barkley's model is a useful formulation of ADHD**

Barkley's model has incorporated each of the major symptoms associated with ADHD into a cohesive syndrome. The model is important as the symptoms generally impair functional behavior for individuals with ADHD. The model is particularly useful in understanding problems associated with motivation, self-sufficiency, and adaptive behavior among these individuals. While much more research is needed to test various components of the model, it is useful in understanding how the myriad of symptoms associated with ADHD may constitute one disorder, and, more importantly, how the symptoms are associated with each other in forming a unified disorder.

## 2.2    Perinatal Factors in ADHD

Researchers have identified several teratogens during the prenatal period that have been associated with the development of ADHD. These include the effects of maternal alcohol use during pregnancy, nicotine use during pregnancy, and low birth weight babies. For instance, Knopik, Sparrow, Madden, Bucholz, Hudziak, Reich et al. (2005) have identified an association between maternal alcohol consumption during pregnancy and the development of ADHD. Fetal alcohol syndrome (FAS) and fetal alcohol effects (FAE) increase the likelihood of ADHD symptoms (Nanson and Hiscock, 1990). In a sample of 1,452 twin pairs aged 5–16, Thapar, Fowler, Rice, Scourfield, van den Bree, Thomas et al. (2003) found that mothers who used tobacco during pregnancy were more likely to have children with ADHD, even when controlling for potentially confounding variables such as social class and birth weight.

**Alcohol and nicotine use during pregnancy may be associated with the development of ADHD**

Some research demonstrates a relation between low birth weight and the development of ADHD (e.g., Breslau, Brown, DelDotto, Kumar, Ezhuthachan, Andreski, & Hufnagle, 1996; Knopik et al., 2005). Data from studies conducted by Whitaker, Van Rossem, Feldman, Schonfeld, Pinto-Martin, Tore et al. (1997) indicate that infants' cranial ultrasound abnormalities are associated with an increase in risk for ADHD at age the age of six years. In 252 children with ADHD and 231 controls, Mick, Biederman, Prince, Fischer, and Faraone (2002) found that individuals with ADHD were three times more likely to have had low birth weights than comparison controls. The researchers controlled for variables such as prenatal exposure to nicotine and alcohol, parental ADHD, and comorbid behavior disorders. Such connections between low birth weight and ADHD, however, are not always replicated (e.g., St. Sauver et al., 2004).

**Many individuals with ADHD had low birth weights**

## 2.3    Psychological Factors in ADHD

A number of environmental factors contribute to the ADHD phenotype. While these agents do not necessarily cause the disorder, they are associated or may exacerbate a constitutional predisposition to the disorder. Theoretical perspectives with environmental components address attachment disorders, levels of familial conflict, caregiver warmth and support, caregiver educational achievement, caregiver substance use, and child abuse trauma. St. Sauver et al. (2004) observed an inverse association between parental education levels and risk for ADHD. Other psychologists have contributed an attachment perspective to conceptualizations of ADHD (e.g., Stiefel, 1997). Erdman (1998) suggests that parent-child attachment patterns contribute to ADHD. Kreppner, O'Connor, Rutter, Beckett, Castle, Croft et al. (2001) found that symptoms of inattention and overactivity were related to disturbed attachment styles. Of course, a very

**Environmental factors exacerbate the predisposition to ADHD**

viable alternative explanation to the attachment theory is that ADHD contributes to an insecure attachment with caregivers.

Several researchers have demonstrated that family dysfunction influences the development of ADHD. Knopik et al. (2005) found that both maternal and paternal alcohol dependency increased the likelihood that children would receive an ADHD diagnosis. Parent-child conflict increases susceptibility for comorbid disorders in childhood that include ADHD (Burt, Krueger, McGue, & Iacono, 2003). Counts, Nigg, Stawicki, Rappley, and von Eye (2005) found that inattention and hyperactivity, as identified by parents and teachers, were independently associated with children's perceptions of marital conflict. In a sample of 335 children affected by parental alcoholism, Jester, Nigg, Adams, Fitzgerald, Puttler, Wong, and Zucker (2005) conducted a longitudinal study demonstrating that low levels of intellectual stimulation and emotional support predicted problems associated with inattention and overactivity.

Child abuse sequelae may include the development of ADHD. Ford, Racusin, Ellis, Daviss, Reiser, Fleischer, and Thomas (2000) reviewed data from 165 consecutive child psychiatric outpatient admissions, and found that ADHD was related to physical or sexual maltreatment. Research demonstrates children may use divided attention to separate distressing information from awareness (Becker-Blease, Freyd, & Pears, 2004). Though this may represent an initially adaptive coping mechanism, it may later predispose individuals to develop attentional difficulties.

**Comorbid psychological disorders can arise from child maltreatment**

Comorbid psychological disorders resulting from childhood maltreatment, such as depression and anxiety, also affect attentional processes. It also must be pointed out that children and adolescents with ADHD are at greater risk for abuse. For example, an impulsive youngster who is gregarious and risk-taking is more apt to be persuaded by an adult to be lured into a situation that places the child or adolescent at risk.

## 2.4    Interactions between Biological and Psychological Factors

There is a general consensus that genetic, environmental, and neurological elements converge to contribute to the presence of ADHD, and it is often difficult to infer causality, especially from cross-sectional studies. For instance, there may be a bi-directional association between family distress and ADHD (Kaplan, Crawford, Fisher, & Dewey, 1998). Tully, Arseneault, Caspi, Moffitt, and Morgan (2004) found that the contributions of low birth weight to ADHD were moderated by maternal warmth. This finding is important as it suggests that environmental factors can mitigate the deleterious effects of specific risk factors that may be associated or even causal in ADHD. On a similar note, Breslau et al. (1996) noted that the association between low birth weight and ADHD was especially significant for those individuals residing in an urban environment relative to those individuals residing in a suburban area of southeast Michigan. Arnsten (1999) has provided a particularly valuable explanation as to the means by which stress may affect the neurochemistry of the prefrontal cortex. The prefrontal cortex is associated with planning and thinking and the control that children may be able to exert over their behaviors. Rickel and Becker-Lausen (1997) provide a visual depiction of the reciprocal interactions between nurturant versus restrictive child rearing practices, other environmental influences, and behavioral outcomes that also include ADHD. The model provided by Rickel and Becker-Lausen is important as it demonstrates the many pathways through which diverse environmental components affect child outcomes.

**Summary**

Some investigators have interpreted all biological disparities between individuals with ADHD relative to comparison controls as evidence of genetic contributions to the disorder. However, there are compelling data to suggest that environmental factors influence developmental neurobiology and accompanying maturational processes. For instance, Rietveld, Hudziak, Bartels, van Beijsterveldt, and Boomsma (2004) have employed data from maternal reports of twin children using the Child Behavior Checklist (CBCL) to demonstrate the heritability of ADHD symptoms and to support a proposed genetic etiology. It is difficult to determine, however, to what extent maternal subjectivity or shared environmental influences might have contributed to such a result. Other studies consider shared features of ADHD among relatives as evidence of a genetic basis, when in fact such commonalities may represent environmental contributions. The research demonstrates that the pathways to ADHD are most likely complex and diverse. It is encouraging that many research endeavors have investigated genetic and environmental contributions concurrently, because this approach will provide the most complete picture of the development of ADHD.

# 3

# Diagnosis and Treatment Indications

Clients present for an ADHD evaluation for a variety of reasons. Very frequently, parents and teachers have concerns regarding children's school performance. Thus, it is not surprising that children are frequently referred for ADHD evaluations when they are in the primary grades of elementary school. When children are referred because of school difficulties, it is usually not possible to determine from the reason for referral whether the impairment will indeed reflect ADHD or another type of generalized or specific learning disability or cognitive disorder (Denckla, 2000). Many adults refer themselves for evaluations after their children receive an ADHD diagnosis, especially when they recognize similar disturbances that they themselves have endured. Adults with ADHD change jobs more frequently, have more trouble completing assignments, and have more difficulty working independently than controls (Weiss & Hechtman, 1986). A common referral issue involves the request to determine whether a child or adult has ADHD, dyslexia, a learning disorder or disorders, or whether multiple diagnoses are most appropriate. Frequently, the clinician's hardest task is to identify a specific diagnosis when confronted with a multitude of possible disorders, or even to identify comorbidities. Many patients who have both ADHD and/or the possibility of another disorder are referred for evaluation by someone who believes they have only ADHD.

**Most diagnoses are made during the elementary school years**

When introducing the ADHD evaluation, it is helpful to explain that everyone has cognitive strengths and areas of difficulty. Though the average age of onset of ADHD is four or five years of age, most children are not diagnosed until problems with academic achievement and social functioning appear during the elementary school years (Shepard, Carter, & Cohen, 2000). This is typically when independent seat-work is required and children with attentional problems encounter difficulties in academic achievement at school. Children who attend preschool may be referred earlier, because social functioning during these years involves cognitive skills such as perspective-taking and emotional regulation, and deficits in these areas may be observed by a teacher. Typically, when ADHD is identified during preschool, it is more severe and the child is more likely to have other comorbidities. ADHD symptoms of inattention and impulsivity may impede appropriate emotional interactions. Day-care situations may include cognitive attentional skills that would otherwise not be a necessary feature of a child's environment.

Assessment can present many challenges. Frequently, individuals with ADHD have limited awareness of their difficulties. They may be either unable to consider their own behavior as abnormal, or may exaggerate symptoms. Often different informants whom the clinician may interview disagree, and they are likely to bring their own biases to the assessment setting. These issues are an important consideration for the evaluating clinician. In addition, a thorough assessment of differential and comorbid conditions is also necessary. Though early diagnosis may increase the likelihood of effective intervention, misdiagnosis may represent a failure to note difficulties with emotional functioning, anxiety, depression, or child abuse.

## 3.1    Assessment Procedures

An ADHD assessment includes the following components: an interview, rating scales or checklists completed by multiple informants for the purpose of capturing a broad perspective with regard to behaviors that may be associated with ADHD across settings, an evaluation of concurrent psychiatric diagnoses, a childhood behavioral and medical history, and neuropsychological testing. While neuropsychological testing does not identify ADHD, it is useful for identifying other comorbidities such as specific learning disabilities. The assessment procedure should be structured according to the age of the client, and the diagnostic process ultimately must include assessing whether or not the client meets criteria according to the DSM-IV-TR formulation.

Clinicians should have an understanding of typical attentional development, emotional regulation, and age-appropriate behaviors. There is a paucity of measures that assess ADHD in preschool children, although many behavioral ratings do provide psychometric data for preschoolers. Therefore, clinicians depend on their ability to compare their clients' behaviors to normative functioning. For preschoolers, diagnostic methods might include naturalistic observations in a structured setting such as in a preschool classroom, standardized interviews and/or self-report questionnaires, and psychological tests (Shepard et al., 2000). It is especially important to investigate the quality of parent-child interactions and family relationships. Parent education about the nature of ADHD, and its management and support, are essential. For evaluations with older children, the interview should include conversations with both children and their parents. When assessing ADHD in adults, it is very helpful to speak with another person who knows the client well, such as a spouse or parent. In order to determine an ADHD diagnosis for adults, there must be a history of impairment during childhood, and supporting documentation if available. Needless to say, the natural history of ADHD is critical in making a diagnosis of the disorder. The disorder must be present from childhood in order to qualify for a diagnosis of ADHD at either adolescence or during adulthood.

In formulating an ADHD diagnosis, the clinician must carefully consider several sources of information. The interview is of central importance in diagnosing ADHD, and in determining its course and gravity. Psychological testing is an additional component, and can supply valuable information regarding the severity of comorbid learning problems. In addition, it is important to have some index of the child's academic functioning in a structured setting in which the child is able to exert her/his best performance. Children and adolescents with ADHD frequently encounter difficulties at school with achievement tests simply due to the fact that they are often administered in a group setting.

**ADHD diagnosis requires an understanding of age-appropriate behavior**

Thus, due to their attentional problems, ADHD children may perform poorly on these tests simply due to the nature of the test administration. Checklists and structured interviews also provide important data, and objective tests are useful because the data they offer are less influenced by biases than are other sources of information. Family members and teachers will each have their own expectations and conceptions of normality. For instance, difficult family relationships can influence perceptions of symptoms.

**Parents and children may have different viewpoints regarding ADHD symptoms**

Clinicians have reported cases in which a child denies the problems that parents have observed. Others have been asked to evaluate children who have no dysfunction other than the inability to meet their parents' inappropriately high standards. It is important to remember that no one instrument is sufficient for a diagnosis (Quinlan, 2000), and a multifaceted approach to assessment has been found to be most useful. Such an approach includes the use of rating scales that assess behavior at home and at school, structured interviews from both parents and teachers that allow for the assessments of symptoms across settings, and finally the use of direct observation in a structured setting where children and adolescents are likely to encounter significant difficulties.

Prior to the administration of any neuropsychological or achievement tests, it is important to ask whether clients have received any stimulant medication or caffeine prior to test administration. Typically, clinicians will ask clients to refrain from taking stimulant medication on the day of testing. For those patients who may be using illegal substances, clinicians report that a period of one month of abstinence is helpful to diagnose ADHD with accuracy (Wilens, Spencer & Biederman, 2000b). For the most accurate reflection of functioning, patients should be cautioned not to consume excessive amounts of caffeine on the day of assessment. Sometimes, an initial test is administered when the client has not taken stimulant medication, followed by a repeat test on a day when the client is medicated. While such a procedure does not constitute a double-blind trial, it does allow for an objective assessment of medication effects with a structured task.

## 3.2     Specific Assessment Techniques

Quinlan (2000) describes four categories of assessment methods: checklists, structured interviews, psychometric tests of cognitive functioning, and instruments that measure specific correlates of ADHD. Since no single method can actually produce a valid diagnosis, as has been noted previously, and a combination of assessment techniques has typically been demonstrated to be the most valid in identifying for ADHD and is therefore recommended.

Brown (1996) provides two versions of a diagnostic form for ADHD: one for adolescents and one for adults. The form assists the clinician to complete a full ADHD assessment, including the interview, rating scales, psychological testing, an assessment of the DSM-IV ADHD symptoms, evaluation of concurrent diagnoses, and feedback to the client. Barkley (1998a) created a four-page self-report questionnaire for assessing adult ADHD that queries clients' developmental, social, health, and employment histories.

Computerized continuous performance tasks (CPTs) have become extremely popular in the assessment of ADHD. With these particular tasks, individuals watch a computer screen and react to a letter or number stimulus by pressing a button. The task measures the ability to sustain attention and effort and the subject's response time. The instruments typically yield errors of omission as well as errors of commission. Individuals with ADHD exhibit lowered sensitivity to stimuli, as represented by unresponsiveness to stimuli or errors of omission (Shepard et al., 2000). Errors of commission are believed to be an index of impulsivity. Losier, McGrath, and Klein (1996) performed a meta-analysis of 26 studies on ADHD, and reported that children with ADHD exhibit a greater number of errors of omission and commission than children without ADHD.

The Conners Continuous Performance Task (CPT; Conners, 1985) is a 14-minute test that involves the presentation of consecutive letters, with a target letter that appears interspersed among six other letters. The stimulus rate varies during the duration of the test, which captures individuals' abilities to process information at different rates. The test provides scores for reaction times, response variability, errors of omission, and errors of commission.

The Test of Variables of Attention (TOVA) (Greenberg & Waldman, 1993), another frequently employed vigilance task that is administered by computer, involves stimuli presented at both infrequent and frequent intervals. Individuals attempt to respond to a target letter that appears intermittently among nontarget letters. The report generated by the TOVA includes scores for response time for correct trials, errors of omission, errors of commission, and anticipatory errors. Clinicians who evaluate these reports assess clients' patterns of errors to gain a sense of inattention and impulsivity (Quinlan, 2000).

The following steps constitute a sample evaluation procedure for adolescents and adults. The process begins with a clinical interview with the persons who may have ADHD. The interview should include several parts:

1. An overview of the presenting problems and their chronology, sources of the referral, a history that includes developmental, medical, academic, and social components, and an evaluation of behaviors intended to compensate for ADHD-related difficulties;

2. An analysis of the ways symptoms may impact school, work, and recreational activities, as well as personal relationships;

3. Collateral interviews with parents or a significant other that include their perspectives on the individuals' symptoms and their impact, and the developmental, medical, and social history of the person who may have ADHD;

4. A psychological evaluation that investigates the presence of Axis II disorders, including the potential presence of mental retardation and developmental disabilities;

5. Self-report measures that include general psychological symptoms, such as the Minnesota Multiphasic Personality Inventory-2 (MMPI-2), the Symptom Checklist-90-Revised (Derogatis, 1975), the Beck Depression Inventory (Beck, 1990), and the Beck Anxiety Inventory (Beck, Steer, & Brown, 1996), as well as ADHD self-report checklists from the Barkley interview (1998a) or the Brown ADD scales (Brown, 1996);

6. A semistructured psychological interview, such as the Barkley clinical interview form or the Brown ADD scales, that evaluates whether the client meets DSM-IV criteria for ADHD (Barkley, 1998a; Brown, 1996);

7. An assessment of cognitive, neuropsychological, and academic functioning that includes the WAIS-III (Wechsler, 1997), the Wechsler Memory Scale-III, reading and mathematics skills, and a continuous performance test such as the Conners CPT or the TOVA.

## 3.3     The Decision-Making Process

**Clinicians need to interpret multiple sources of information to arrive at a diagnosis**

Clinicians should evaluate all of the information they gather during the assessment process to determine whether there is consistent evidence that a client in fact meets the criteria for a diagnosis of ADHD. An important consideration is that the symptoms are cross-situational (e.g., they occur both at home and at school) and that they are verified across all settings (e.g., home and school). The evaluation of neuropsychological tests often involves comparing individuals' performance on intelligence tests with tests designed to assess neurocognitive functioning. As noted previously, when a neuropsychological test battery fails to identify attentional problems, this does not necessarily rule out the presence of ADHD. Given that the assessment setting is a rather contrived environment in which the individual is receiving individualized attention for performance, attentional problems are frequently not revealed in such settings and as a result there are frequently many false negatives in identifying attentional problems. Despite this, the psychological evaluation is frequently useful in identifying comorbidities as well as other emotional stressors that may exacerbate ADHD. Finally, it should be noted that some individuals may fall short of meeting diagnostic criteria for the disorder by one or two symptoms. This puts the clinical psychologist in a dilemma since "subthreshold" ADHD (i.e., situations in which one of two symptoms are missing, thereby failing to qualify a child as meeting specific diagnostic criteria) also may require treatment, despite the fact that the symptoms are not all-encompassing.

## 3.4     Treatment Considerations

**It is important to establish a continuum of care for the individual diagnosed with ADHD**

If an individual is diagnosed with ADHD, the primary aim of treatment should be coordination of resources across settings to establish a continuum of care. The first step should be identifying an appropriate therapist who can advocate the client's needs in the school, work, and family environments. It is helpful for the therapist to collaborate with a physician or psychologist who is able to prescribe medication if this is deemed to be necessary.

Individuals with ADHD are often referred because of a co-occurring disorder, including learning problems, mood disorders, anxiety disorders, posttraumatic stress disorder, obsessive-compulsive disorder, or conduct disorder. When children have comorbid ADHD and learning disorders, academic adjustments are often necessary. These can include alternative classroom

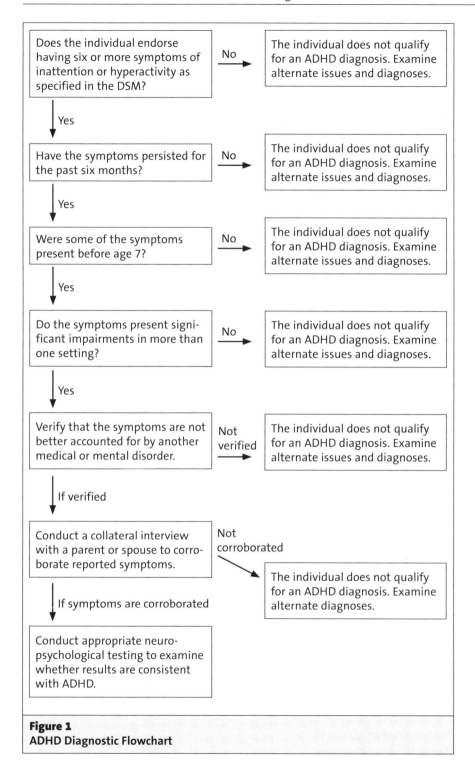

**Figure 1**
**ADHD Diagnostic Flowchart**

formats, help with study skills and organization, and increased time for tests. Other types of accommodations or services may also be necessary, including special education services either within a self-contained classroom or within a resource setting (e.g., part-time special education services for specific academic areas). If a patient is actively abusing substances, it may be important to address the immediate problem of addiction, which may require medical treatments, followed by ongoing psychotherapy for the substance abuse.

After ADHD and potential comorbid disorders have been evaluated, providers should develop an intervention plan. In most cases of childhood ADHD, clinicians will collaborate with the student, teachers, and parents to create an individualized educational plan (IEP). Even though psychosocial interventions are frequently recommended as complements to stimulant medication, psychopharmacological treatments often are the only treatments received by individuals with ADHD due to the fact that many children and adolescents have poor access to mental health services.

Psychoeducational components are often a key element of success, and clients, parents or family members may need to be trained in the most effective ways to advocate for those with ADHD. Interventions can include special accommodations for students with ADHD, such as classroom formats with increased variation and interaction, additional time for tests and papers, tutoring, and instruction regarding specific note-taking and study techniques.

### Summary

It is critical that clinicians establish positive rapport with clients and their families, and aim for a relationship that emphasizes collaboration. Both clinicians and clients must employ interventions that are evidence based, although they still need to keep in mind that every individual is unique, and responses to interventions will vary. All approaches should be carefully monitored to promote compliance and the greatest likelihood of benefits.

# 4

# Treatment

## 4.1 Methods of Treatment

While ADHD is a chronic neurodevelopment disorder that often carries a somewhat guarded prognosis (Barkley et al., 2005), there are several well-researched treatment approaches for the disorder, many of which are evidenced-based. Because of the heterogeneity of symptoms and needs among those with the disorder, it is likely that different treatment plans will be appropriate for different patients. In addition, recent research suggests that specific therapies work best for ADHD when it is comorbid with other psychiatric disorders. When choosing a treatment plan, it is often helpful for parents, teachers, and families to pinpoint specific behaviors and challenges to address. Once these goals are identified, it is easier to assess whether specific interventions are effective. Treatment methods may include stimulant medication, psychoeducational interventions, behavioral therapies and a combination of two or more of these approaches.

### 4.1.1 Stimulant Medication

Stimulants are one of the most frequently prescribed and researched psychotropics in the field of child and adolescent psychiatry. There is a documented increase in the use of stimulant medication for children and adolescents with ADHD that has been attributed to better identification of the disorder, a recognition that there are specific subgroups of the disorder, and finally, the fact that there is poor access to mental health services, particularly among those individuals who have no insurance.

**Studies show that stimulant medication is effective in enhancing concentration**

Before discussing specific stimulant medications with clients and their families, it is important to address their understanding and expectations regarding stimulants and their effects, and to provide psychoeducation about the benefits as well as the potential adverse side effects of these agents. Individuals exhibit a range of responses to medications. Stimulant medications have been demonstrated to improve some of the specific symptoms associated with ADHD. In particular, stimulants have been demonstrated to be effective in enhancing attention and concentration for individuals with ADHD.

Unfortunately, stimulants do not enhance all of the functional outcomes associated with the ADHD disorder, including problems with social behavior and academic performance. With some of the newer stimulants, research has generally suggested that approximately 90% of children and adolescents respond to the stimulants (American Academy of Pediatrics, 2000), although other classes of psychotropics may prove more effective for ADHD when it is comorbid with anxiety disorder or depression. Finally, stimulants may be contraindicated in some children and adolescents (e.g., in families in which there is a member with a substance abuse disorder).

**Stimulant medication may be inappropriate for children under the age of five**

For preschoolers, there has been considerable debate in the clinical literature regarding the potential safety and efficacy of stimulant medications for preschoolers. Frequently, children under the age of five years experience a host of adverse effects associated with stimulants. To provide a greater evidence base regarding the safety and efficacy of the stimulants, a large-scale clinical trial sponsored by the National Institutes of Health is underway to systematically study the safety and efficacy of the stimulants among preschoolers. Since the prefrontal cortex is not fully developed in young children, and stimulants generally exert their effects in this region of the brain, it is unclear if they are helpful for this young patient population given that organs that metabolize stimulants are also immature. Furthermore, a primary target behavior in prescribing the stimulants is to improve school performance by increasing attention and concentration. Because preschool children are not in a traditional classroom setting, use of medication may not be necessary for the purpose of enhancing functional outcomes in this age group, including attention and concentration (Shepard et al., 2000).

There has been considerable research to demonstrate that stimulant medications exert positive effects on the core symptoms of ADHD, particularly attention. For example, research has demonstrated that individuals make fewer errors on the CPT when treated with methylphenidate (Quinlan, 2000). While stimulants appear to improve social functioning, these effects, albeit statistically significant, have not always been clinically significant (Tannock & Brown, 2000). However, few studies have demonstrated the effects of stimulant medication on functional components of the disorder, including academic achievement. Although the majority of clinical trials examining the efficacy of the stimulants have included Caucasian males as participants, some recent investigations have included females as well as participants from various ethnic groups (Arnold, 1997; Pelham, 1993). Findings have generally suggested comparable response among these individuals relative to their male Caucasian peers.

**Special care is suggested when prescribing stimulant medication to patients with dual diagnosis**

Research has evaluated the effectiveness of stimulant medication for ADHD when there are comorbid diagnoses including mood disorders and anxiety disorders. The findings of these investigations have generally suggested that response to stimulant medications are compromised (Spencer, Wilens, Biederman, Wozniak, & Harding-Crawford, 2000). Two studies (Gammon & Brown, 1993; Findling, 1996) suggest that combining specific serotonin reuptake inhibitors (SSRIs) and stimulant medications is safe and effective; however, other reports caution that SSRIs may not be effective for ADHD (Wilens et al., 2000b). For clients with substance abuse disorders, stimulant medication can reduce cravings for substances (e.g., Riggs, Thompson, Mikulich, Whitmore, & Crowley, 1996), although stimulants should be used with caution when treating patients who have a history of substance abuse. Contrary to popular opinion, the use of stimulant medication during childhood has been shown to reduce the risk for substance abuse in adulthood (Barkley et al., 2005; Biederman, Wilens, Mick, Spencer, & Faraone, 1999). Clinicians should actively monitor the response to medication in all patients, and should proceed with special care in the case of dual diagnoses, particularly substance abuse.

All medication effects must be carefully monitored by clinicians. Brown (2000) notes that many patients provide general descriptions of medication response, and advises that they need to receive instructions in reporting more specific reactions, particularly adverse effects. Clinicians should also be sensitive to the potential demand characteristics that accompany the positions of authority held by health professionals.

**Use of stimulant medication must be carefully monitored for side effects**

Clients who do not observe benefits from one stimulant medication may respond to another. A meta-analysis of 23 studies that compared stimulant medications revealed few differences between methylphenidate, dexedrine, and pemoline, the primary stimulants used to manage ADHD (McMaster University Evidence-Based Practice Center Group, 1999).

Adverse side effects from stimulant medication may include decreased appetite, motor tics, sleep problems, headaches, stomach pain, nausea, fatigue, and irritability. Many side effects associated with stimulants may abate after a short period, or may disappear if the dosage or timing of administration is adjusted (McMaster University Evidence-Based Practice Center Group, 1999).

The most commonly used stimulant medications include methylphenidate (Ritalin), dextroamphetamine (Dexedrine), dextroamphetamine and amphetamine combined (Adderall), and pemoline (Cylert). Brief descriptions of these specific drugs follow below. It is important to note that many of these agents also come in extended release forms making once daily dosing possible, eliminating the need for multiple daily dosing.

Methylphenidate (Ritalin) comes in 5, 10, and 20 mg tablets, and lasts between three and four hours. The effects of the medication are usually observed in about half an hour. The medication should be started at a low dose, and increased slowly over a four to five week period. Methylphenidate also is available in a sustained release preparation in 20 mg tablets. Some reports indicate that the sustained release medication may be less effective; however, many patients have been reported to perform well on the longer-acting medication, particularly when evaluated with behavioral ratings.

Dextroamphetamine (Dexedrine) is sold in 5 mg tablets, which roughly corresponds to 10 mg of methylphenidate. The beneficial effects of dextroamphetamine generally last approximately four hours. The medication should be introduced at a low dose, and the dosage should be increased over a four week period. Dexedrine is available in a timed release form known as the Dexedrine Spansule. This preparation lasts approximately eight to ten hours, and may be useful for clients where multiple doses throughout the day may pose difficulties or where adherence to medication is uncertain.

Adderall is a compound of dextroamphetamine and amphetamine. It is available in tablets of 5, 10, 20, and 30 mg, and its effects last between six to eight hours. The mixture, which includes salt compounds, prolongs the effectiveness of the drug. Some reports indicates that Adderall may be appropriate for clients who are unresponsive to other drug therapy for ADHD (e.g., Pliszka, Borcherding, Spratley, Leon, & Irick, 1997).

Pemoline (Cylert) is available in 37.5 mg tablets, and may also be an option for clients who are not responsive to methylphenidate or dextroamphetamine. There may be an association between pemoline and liver failure, as cases have been reported in children and adults (Safer, Zito, & Gardner, 2001). Abbott Laboratories, the company that manufactures the drug, recommend that pemoline not be used as the first-line medication of choice for ADHD.

More recently atomoxetine (Strattera) has been used for the management of ADHD. Atomoxetine affects the transmitters of norepinephrine and is not classified as a stimulant, although it does have stimulant effects. It is usually taken either once or twice daily. It is the only medication that has received approval from the FDA to treat adult ADHD (Spencer, 2004).

Another recent psychotropic therapy for ADHD is modafinil (Provigil), which is a cognitive enhancement agent primarily used to promote wakefulness. Modafinil differs structurally from other drugs for ADHD, and selectively targets the cerebral cortex (Biederman et al., 2005). It has been prescribed as an off-label treatment for ADHD (Rugino & Samsock, 2003). Modafinil is usually administered once daily, with dosage levels of approximately 170–425 mg.

**Patient response to stimulant medication varies, and an individuals response should be carefully monitored**

Individual responses to stimulant medication are quite variable, and health professionals and patients should carefully evaluate patients' responses to these medication. Stimulants should be carefully and gradually titrated so that an optimal dose is reached, i.e., one which manages specific target behaviors (e.g., teacher ratings of inattention) while still resulting in the fewest adverse effects. The dose is at an appropriate level when maximum benefits can be observed, and adverse side effects are at a minimum. During the titration period, the medication should be used for seven days, so that changes can be observed across a range of environments. During this period, patients and family members should attempt to observe the effects of medication throughout each day, and compare these observations with the structure of environmental demands. It is especially useful to note the times of day where effects of medication begin to wear off, and to attempt to have these times correspond to recreation or mealtimes or other situation where high levels of concentration are not essential. In addition, ingesting stimulants with meals or snacks can help alleviate some common side effects, such as gastrointestinal inflammation.

**Drug holidays are recommended to evaluate the need for medication and to inhibit tolerance to stimulants**

It is recommended that prescribing physicians monitor medication effects weekly during the titration period, and monthly once medications are stable. Periodically (at least once a year), patients should attempt to take a "drug holiday" to reevaluate the need for medication and to inhibit the development of tolerance to stimulants. For children with ADHD, drug holidays are generally taken during the summer months, and the child is encouraged to return to school in September without medication. This provides the opportunity for parents and practitioners to obtain a baseline of behavior prior to readministering the medication at the beginning of the school year. Drug holidays are contraindicated if patients are in the midst of stressful circumstances, or if discontinuation of the medication could precipitate dangers such as accidents or abuse (Weiss et al., 1999).

Studies that have examined the effects of stimulant medications have generally shown that there are no differences between the various agents (for a review, see Brown & Sammons, 2003) and that if a child fails to respond to one of the stimulant agents, he or she will likely respond to another stimulant (for review see Brown et al., 2006).

Some individuals with ADHD are treated with medications initially developed for other psychiatric populations. Patients may be prescribed tricyclic antidepressants (TCAs), including imipramine (Tofranil), nortryptaline (Pamelor), and desipramine (Norpramine). Other physicians prescribe bupropion (Wellbutrin) or clonidine (Catapres). Researchers are currently investigating whether modafinil (Provigil) may be appropriate for individuals with ADHD. For patients with comorbid diagnoses, particularly comorbidity of the internalizing disorders (e.g., anxiety disorders or depression) or for those few individuals who do not respond to stimulant medications, other psychotropic medications are often prescribed. These may include medications that target depression, anxiety, or mood lability. Though many stimulant medications involve multiple dosages throughout the day, timed-release medications options require fewer doses to achieve consistent effects.

For children with ADHD, medication decisions should be reached through collaboration between parents, teachers, and medical personnel. Before anyone begins a medication regimen, he or she should undergo a physical evaluation that assesses height, weight, pulse, and blood pressure in order to determine whether there are any pre-existing medical conditions. If a physician is considering prescribing Cylert, they should evaluate the individual for a baseline of liver functioning, since Cylert is associated with impaired hepatic function. When patients begin taking medications for ADHD, they should begin with a small dose of the drug (typically 5 mg), and gradually increase the dose. Though the doses for medication tablets usually last four hours, this may vary among patients, and may range from 2.5–4 hours. Based on each person's specific response to the medication, patients and health professionals can determine the dose that is best suited to the patient for the specific target symptoms being addressed. In the weeks and months following the commencement of drug treatment, individuals should monitor and evaluate ADHD symptoms and adverse side effects in collaboration with families, teachers, clinicians, and appropriate peers. Measures to assess patients' responses to medication should be similar to those assessments used to diagnose and identify specific target behaviors for which the medication may be intended.

It is also important that the child's privacy and confidentiality be protected when children require the administration of ADHD medications during school hours. Medication management should include careful monitoring and follow-up attention by medical doctors, psychologists, teachers, and family to address side effects and the effect on ADHD symptoms. Frequently multiple dosing of medication during the school hours is difficult and many children, and especially adolescents may find this to be stigmatizing. Hence those preparations of stimulants that are made for longer duration of action may be most appropriate for these children and adolescents.

## 4.1.2    Psychotherapy

In addition to pharmacotherapy, there are several forms of psychotherapy that may be useful for individuals with ADHD. Furthermore, because many individuals with ADHD also have other psychological symptoms that may include depression or aggression, therapy can address aspects of functioning that may not be responsive to stimulant medication. Therapy can also target issues com-

**Psychotherapy may be useful for individuals with ADHD**

mon to individuals with ADHD, such as low self-esteem and self-efficacy. It can also address the marital and family conflict often associated with adults who have ADHD. Many forms of intervention emphasize psychoeducational approaches. In addition to providing psychotherapy, many healthcare professionals may refer their patients to helpful books, videotapes, or internet sites that provide accessible information regarding the etiology and treatment of ADHD. A number of these resources are included in Chapter 8.

Many individuals with ADHD, especially those without early intervention, have had to endure others' assessments of them as "lazy," "ineffective," "mentally compromised," or "unfocused." Others may have recognized their functional deficits and attributed these impairments to inherent characteristics. Since individuals affected by ADHD have often internalized these negative messages, psychological interventions can help target and correct these inaccurate judgments and their effects on self-schemas. While cognitive therapy may help reduce these negative thoughts and their accompanying dysphoric emotions, generally cognitive therapy as a medium for reducing the cognitive impairments associated with the ADHD disorder has not been demonstrated to be efficacious (for review, see Gittelman and Abikoff, 1989).

In other cases, psychotherapy may address specific hardships influenced by ADHD, such as difficulties at school or work. Behavior management techniques are often helpful, especially for younger children (Brown, 2000), and have been demonstrated to be the therapy of choice in the management of symptoms of ADHD as well as associated functional impairments. In addition, individuals with ADHD may have relationships that are compromised by the disorder. ADHD symptoms often provoke family conflict, or constitute a challenge for maintaining friendships and partner relationships. ADHD can affect parenting skills, and parents with this disorder may require psychoeducation and monitoring to ensure they are parenting in a conscientious and consistent manner. Clinicians should carefully consider how the family environment and other relational networks may alleviate or exacerbate attention and hyperactivity symptoms.

**Behavioral techniques that reinforce positive behavior, applied in the classroom or at home, have been found to be very effective**

Behavioral techniques are commonly used for individuals with ADHD and have been demonstrated as the psychotherapy of choice for the disorder because of their firm evidence-base in the extant literature. Behavior therapy may be helpful in its emphasis on structure and its reinforcement of positive behaviors. Behavior therapy can include interventions that are taught to parents and teachers. Children may demonstrate the greatest degree of behavior change when they receive consistent responses for their actions. Methods of behavior therapy include management skills for parents and teachers, contingency management (such as "time outs" and positive reinforcement), and training that targets social skills and problem-solving. Consistency and follow-up are important components of successful treatment with behavior therapy.

Table 3 illustrates some of the behavioral techniques that may be helpful for children with ADHD. It is reprinted with permission from Rieff and Tippins (2004).

Over the past three decades numerous studies have demonstrated that behavioral interventions are associated with the reduction of symptoms and functional impairments related to ADHD. In fact, it has been suggested that the effects of tightly controlled behavior management are equivalent with

**Table 3:**
**Effective behavioral techniques for children with ADHD**

| Technique | Description | Example |
|---|---|---|
| Positive reinforcement | Providing rewards or privileges dependent on the child's performance. | Child completes an assignment and is permitted to play on the computer. |
| Time out | Removing access to positive reinforcement contingent on performance of unwanted or problem behavior. | Child hits sibling impulsively and is required to sit for 5 minutes in the corner of the room. |
| Response cost | Withdrawing rewards or privileges contingent on the performance of unwanted or problem behavior. | Child loses free-time privileges for not completing homework. |
| Token economy | The child earns rewards and privileges contingent on performing desired behaviors. This type of positive reinforcement can be combined with response cost, where a child can also lose the rewards and privileges based on undesirable behavior. | Child earns stars for completing assignments and loses stars for getting out of seat. Child cashes in stars at the end of the week for a prize. |

low to moderate doses of stimulant medication (for review, see Pelham & Wasenbusch, 1999). By contrast to studies of stimulant medication, studies of behavioral treatments have focused on functional impairments associated with ADHD. These effects are believed to mediate the long-term outcomes associated with ADHD including parent practices, peer relationships, and school functioning (for review see Brown, Antonuccio, DuPaul, Fristad, King, Leslie et al., in press). Behavioral therapies for children and adolescents with ADHD have been studied in behavioral parent training (Anastopoulos, Shelton, & Barkley, 2005), academic and behavioral classroom interventions (DuPaul & Stoner, 2003), and interventions for peer problems (Mrug, Hoza, & Gerdes, 2001). Behavioral interventions have been systematically examined across the developmental spectrum ranging from preschoolers to adolescence, although clearly much more research is needed with adolescents with ADHD (for a review, see Brown et al., in press).

## Parent Training

A number of studies have examined behavioral parent training including, compliance with parental requests, rule-following, defiant and aggressive behavior, as well as symptoms associated with ADHD (Anastopoulos, Shelton, DuPaul, & Guevremont, 1993). After several months of intervention, findings have generally revealed moderate to large effect sizes (Brown et al., in press). In particular larger effects have been demonstrated on functional outcomes than on specific symptoms of ADHD as delineated in the DSM-IV-TR. Moreover, the effects of parent training have been found to be greatest in the presence of comorbid diagnoses (Hartman, Stage, & Webster-Stratton, 2003; Jensen, Hinshaw, Kraemer, Lenora, Newcorn, Abikoff et al., 2001; Lundahl, Risser, & Lovejoy, 2006). In fact, behavioral parent training has been demonstrated to be one of the most well-validated interventions in the field of childhood psychopathology, particularly for children with aggression and conduct problems (Brestan & Eyberg, 1998). Studies have generally demonstrated similar changes among younger children and adolescents (for review, see Brown et al., in press).

### School-Based Interventions

Classroom behavioral interventions have been widely researched over the past 30 years, and there is compelling evidence attesting to the efficacy of these behavioral approaches in the classroom setting (Brown et al., in press). A number of techniques are available for classroom use including the Daily Report Cards (DRC), as well as token and point systems. Again, consistent with parent behavioral approaches, classroom behavioral interventions studies have typically targeted symptoms associated with ADHD as well as functional impairments such as disobeying classroom rules, disruptive behavior, failing to comply with teacher requests, and not getting along with other classmates. The effects of such interventions in special education settings in which the programs are intensive have generally revealed greater effects than in traditional classroom settings (for review see, Brown et al., in press).

Similarly, a number of studies have focused on academic interventions in classrooms that have included target behaviors such as seatwork productivity and accuracy of academic outcomes (DuPaul & Eckert, 1997; Brown et al., in press). In general these studies have focused on specific daily classroom functioning that is conducive to academic success (e.g., academic productivity, on task behavior) rather than academic achievement that has been assessed over the course of time. Academic strategies may result in behavior change that is consistent with contingency management where target symptoms are more specific to behavioral functioning (DuPaul & Eckert, 1997). In single-subject designs, contingency management approaches also have been demonstrated to enhance academic activities of both elementary school-aged children as well as their adolescent counterparts, although these effects must be replicated in larger group design studies.

### Peer Interventions

**Social skills training can augment school- and home-based interventions**

Peer interventions have generally focused on teaching social skills, social problem-solving, enhancing behavioral competencies, and decreasing aggression as well as other undesirable social behaviors (e.g., controlling behavior, bullying). Frequently, such interventions are applied in school-based social skills groups, weekend groups, as well as summer camp programs (e.g., Pelham,

Fabiano, Gnagy, Greiner, Hoza, Manos, & Janakovic, 2005). Frequently, these programs are used simultaneously with parent training, school-based interventions, or their combination (for review see, Brown et al., in press). There is preliminary evidence that weekly social skills groups may augment the effects of school-based and home-based interventions (Pfiffner & McBurnett, 1997), and there is compelling evidence attesting to the efficacy of peer interventions that are delivered simultaneously with other behavioral approaches including parent training and classroom training (Pelham, Burrows-MacLean, Gnagy, Fabiano, Coles, Tesco et al., 2005). Findings from the MTA study that involved a combination of parent training, teacher consultation and a summer camp program that focused on peer interventions (Wells, Pelham, Kotkin, Hoza, Abikoff, Abramowitz et al., 2000) revealed large pre- to post-test improvements that were sustained at the two-year follow-up assessment (MTA Cooperative Group, 2004).

### Summary of Behavioral Interventions

Results of literature reviews and meta-analyses have generally revealed effect sizes for behavior management programs to be in the moderate to large range. Methods used include parent training and school-based studies; single subject designs have demonstrated even larger effect sizes. Consistent with medication for children and adolescents with ADHD, behavioral therapies have had little impact on academic achievement in the long-term. As Brown et al. (in press) have pointed out, however, when academic achievement has been assessed, there are few studies that have lasted long enough to realistically influence long-term academic achievement.

As Brown et al. (in press) have argued, while there is compelling evidence that behavioral interventions for ADHD are effective, they also have limitations. These limitations include:

1. the fact that they do not work to the same degree for all children and adolescents and that they are not sufficient for some children;
2. the interventions are frequently labor intensive and thus may be more expensive than medication alone in the short-term;
3. behavioral interventions have greater demonstrated evidence for acute than for long-term effects; and finally,
4. behavioral interventions must be implemented simultaneously across settings and domains including home, school, and among peers (for a review, see Brown et al., in press).

It should be noted that the majority of these limitations apply to pharmacotherapy as well, and given the limitations of pharmacotherapy and behavioral approaches, many experts have decided that combined interventions are the most effective for the management of ADHD symptoms and functional impairments and hence should be routinely employed for the management of ADHD.

## 4.1.3    Combined Pharmacological and Behavioral Interventions

A number of investigations have examined combined interventions in special classroom settings and summer treatment programs, as well as in regular class-

**Behavioral interventional can lower the necessary stimulant dosage**

room and in home settings (for a review see, Brown et al., in press). Carlson and her associates (Carlson, Pelham, Milich, & Dixon, 1992) found that the effects of a behavioral intervention and a relatively low dose of stimulant medication were equivalent on several dependent measures of behavioral functioning. More importantly, Carlson et al. (1992) found that the combination of behavior management and stimulant medication was equivalent to a treatment of a high dose of stimulant medication used alone. In a recent extension of this finding, Pelham, Burrows-MacLean et al. (2005) found that very low doses of stimulant medication in combination with behavior therapy maximized efficacy in a combined treatment program. Lower doses of medication provided better acute efficacy, and there were fewer adverse side effects associated with the lower doses of stimulant medication than with the higher doses.

**Combined treatment techniques are most effective, especially for children with comorbid disorders**

In the National Institute's of Health Multimodal Treatment for ADHD study, four treatments were examined including medication, community treatment alone, behavior therapy, and the combination of behavior therapy and medication. Large improvements were demonstrated from baseline to follow-up evaluation with few differences between the four treatment groups. However, later follow-up analyses revealed that the combination of treatments was superior to medication alone on the majority of dependent measures. Moreover, the combination of therapies was especially superior for children with comorbid disorders and for those children with impairments in multiple domains. Further, the study medication and behavioral treatment arm also received greater consumer satisfaction ratings among parents and caregivers (Conners, 2001; MTA Cooperative Group, 1999b). It also should be noted that at the ten-month follow-up assessment, combined treatment was found to be superior to behavior therapy only on symptoms associated with ADHD and oppositional defiant disorder (ODD), and not on the other domains of functioning including parent-child relationships, academic achievement, and social skills. Finally, at the two-year follow-up evaluation, findings revealed that when the medication was withdrawn from the follow-up assessment, the effects of the medication dissipated, although the behavioral effects of the medication still sustained.

Cognitive methods problem-solving techniques, self-monitoring of thoughts and behaviors, and enhanced awareness of the causes and consequences of behaviors. Cognitive approaches address the self-schemas and core beliefs that individuals with ADHD may have developed. Those who have heard themselves described as lazy, irresponsible, or unintelligent may have internalized these messages to the point where they impact many thoughts and behaviors. Through understanding these patterns of thought and their relation to moods and behaviors, clinicians and patients can work together to establish more accurate and beneficial thinking, which in turn affects other elements of functioning. In addition, monitoring the effects of successful behavioral interventions can help convince individuals with ADHD that they are capable and responsible, and this evidence can assist clients to challenge some of their distressing negative beliefs. Typically, cognitive approaches could be most appropriate for adults with ADHD who have internalized feelings of demoralization commonly associated with the disorder. Cognitive therapy may prove useful for some individuals who experience issues related to having a life-long psychiatric disorder that is especially stigmatizing.

Cognitive therapy processes may appear to be well-suited to individuals with ADHD who have some degree of insight into their difficulties. This therapy emphasizes awareness of attentional patterns and interventions that may help change the direction, processes, and content of people's thinking. In addition, cognitive-behavioral treatment often includes homework assignments, which can provide challenges and opportunities for growth. Clients and therapists can use homework assignments to evaluate obstacles to task completion and evidence that supports or refutes core beliefs, and to strategize which methods are most effective. Since cognitive therapy demands some degree of sophistication in terms of being conscious of one's thought processes, it may be most appropriate for adolescents or adults.

**Adolescents and adults are most likely to benefit from cognitive therapy, while family therapy is a helpful intervention for children with ADHD**

Family therapy is often a helpful intervention for children with ADHD. Therapists should emphasize that many behaviors demonstrated by children with ADHD stem from the disorder. Parents are a critical part of the encouragement that is necessary for children to develop self-esteem and effective methods for coping with ADHD. At the same time, every child is different, and not every behavior is attributable to ADHD. Furthermore, parents are likely to have additional issues besides their child's ADHD. These factors affect their child's experience and the family's management of ADHD. When it seems clear to the clinician that parents' own issues are impeding the progress of family therapy, the clinician may recommend individual or couples' therapy to address relevant concerns that are not specifically related to ADHD. In addition, there are a number of strategic family approaches available that make heavy use of behavior management within the context of a family systems approach (Robin, 1988; for review see Barkley, 2006).

Pisterman, McGrath, Firestone, Goodman, Webster, & Mallory (1989) developed an intervention program designed to assist preschoolers with ADHD (ages three to six) and their parents. The parent-training program included 12 sessions. The first three sessions addressed the theories and the course of ADHD, as well as behavior management and important issues in parent-child relationships. The next eight sessions were allocated towards the development of parenting skills, and included instruction regarding appropriate responses to desirable and undesirable behaviors, and the use of effective disciplinary practices such as time outs. This approach mirrors those that have been employed for school-aged children and adolescents, and is generally found to be successful for the management of ADHD within a family systems framework.

Successful interventions that involve parents, emphasize the need for structure and routine in children's lives. Parents can influence children's success at school by helping children with strategies to record and complete homework assignments, keeping school papers in appropriate folders or binders, and setting specific times for homework and studying. In other situations, parents can have children repeat back instructions that are especially important to ensure comprehension. Appropriate discipline needs to reflect this consistency, and concrete rewards and consequences need to be the standard in parents' management of behavior. Parents need to avoid ineffective discipline techniques, such as administering punishment without advance warning or without the child's understanding of the consequences. It is critical that parents respond consistently to undesirable behaviors.

### 4.1.4    Common Psychological Issues with Adults

Adults with ADHD may not understand their disorder or its impact on their lives. Although this understanding may vary with every patient, they often reflect some common themes. Some patients may be unaware of the extent to which ADHD affects the dynamics of their lives, including interpersonal relationships and career development. For example, many adults with ADHD have marital difficulties that eventually lead to divorce, and many adults with ADHD frequently have lower paying jobs than their peers who do not suffer from the disorder. Many individuals develop coping mechanisms that include avoiding tasks that they find challenging because of their ADHD symptoms. Others may attribute most of their difficulties in life to the disorder, and adopt a victim mentality. Adults who have ADHD may have conflicted perceptions regarding stimulant medication. While some may eschew psychotropic medications, others may view medication as a panacea for their problems, and in doing so they may neglect to attend to other aspects of functioning that may require interventions other than stimulant therapy.

Adults with recent diagnoses of ADHD also find themselves in a position of rethinking their own and others' views of their character and functioning. Many individuals may have been told that they are lazy, irresponsible, or incompetent, and could experience distress as they re-evaluate their self-perceptions and feelings towards those who provided such feedback. Adults who have been diagnosed recently with ADHD may experience a sense of loss after thinking about aspects of their lives that may have been different had they received the diagnosis earlier in their development. Still others may regret that their lives have not developed in the ways they had envisioned. Communicating sensitivity and a willingness to explore the veracity and meaning of these interpretations will help therapists to establish rapport and understand their patients' experiences.

The symptoms related to ADHD should help inform therapists regarding the structure and content of therapy for adults with the disorder. Difficulties with attention and organization can result in adult patients with ADHD missing appointments, forgetting information, and demonstrating a lack of follow-through on therapy assignments. Although there is little research that documents the effectiveness of various therapeutic approaches for the management of ADHD in adulthood (e.g., pharmacotherapy versus psychotherapy or their combination), most clinicians agree that structured therapy formats are more suitable than methods that involve free-association. Therapists and clients can collaborate to determine the structure that is most appropriate to the patient's needs, and such discussions can provide useful material for examining clients' strengths and weaknesses and for problem-solving around relevant symptoms.

When treating patients with ADHD it is important to avoid the error of parsimony, as these individuals may have issues that are unrelated to the disorder. Conversely, if clinicians are not attuned to the ways ADHD may affect the therapeutic relationship, even the most experienced clinician could attribute ADHD-related behaviors to resistance, avoidance, or other characteristics that can reinforce painful messages clients with ADHD receive from others around them. All behaviors that occur within the therapeutic setting, including the potential misunderstandings that can arise within the therapeutic dyads, can be used as material for exploration and increased knowledge.

Ramsay and Rostain (2005) identify several aspects of psychotherapy that should be modified for adults with ADHD. Psychoeducation is an important element of therapy for clients with these disorders. In addition to the psycho-educational components that comprise part of therapy sessions for all individuals, therapists can refer clients to appropriate books and websites, including those identified in the Resource section of the book.

Ramsay and Rostain (2005) assert that when clients discuss difficulties arising from their ADHD symptoms, they should be encouraged to supply detailed examples that can be used for illustrating and problem-solving their difficulties. These examples may subsequently be used for considering plans for coping with challenging situations in the future. Elements of cognitive therapy, such as conceptualizing ADHD-related schemas and beliefs, attention to compensatory strategies, and evaluating avoidant behaviors may be especially helpful for adults with ADHD. Murphy (2005) highlights the importance of cultivating hope in adults with ADHD, as many patients may harbor feelings of hopelessness regarding their potential for success and efficacy across several domains in their lives including their employment, marriages, and personal relationships.

## Work-Related Concerns

Nadeau (2005) addresses the career and work issues that affect adults with ADHD. Surprisingly, to date the psychological literature on ADHD has devoted little attention to this important area. Nadeau believes it is important for psychologists to address this issue when engaged in psychotherapy with individuals with ADHD. Specifically, Nadeau has suggested that cognitive and neuropsychological perspectives should be incorporated into their practices and also has recommended offering career-related advocacy and guidance. As ADHD progresses throughout the lifespan, individuals often become less hyperactive, but retain difficulties with attention and concentration. Problems with executive function can often interfere with work-related success. Adults with ADHD may exhibit impairments with time management, organization, and prioritization. As a result may these issues cause adults with ADHD to have unsatisfactory work performances with resultant feelings of being overwhelmed or out of control, and associated feelings of low self-efficacy, low self-esteem, and even learned helplessness (Nadeau, 2005).

**ADHD often impacts adults' work and career**

There are several factors that may contribute to workplace and career success for individuals with ADHD. These include jobs that present a good fit with the individual's strengths, and the ability to integrate compensatory strategies into preexisting job requirements. Nadeau (2005) recommends that clinicians conduct an assessment of their patients' careers and workplaces. Nadeau details the components of such an assessment, which should include an analysis of clients' employment histories, current and past workplace issues, relationships with superiors and coworkers, and ADHD symptoms that may affect work performance and relationships. Murphy (2005) also describes the elements of such an evaluation, and adds questions regarding patients' "passions, interests, aptitudes, likes, and skills." (p. 613). Investigations of appropriate employment may also include career measures or inventories. For their adult clients, psychologists also should encourage cognitive techniques such as reframing their challenges as strengths and encouraging their motivation and the pursuit of their goals (Nadeau, 2005).

The Americans with Disabilities Act (ADA) declares that individuals with disabilities, including ADHD, have a legal right to obtain accommodations suitable to their specific needs. To receive these accommodations, individuals need to make their employers or agencies aware of their disability. Murphy (2005) notes that the decision to inform colleagues and superiors about the disorder is a very personal one, and it may elicit both costs and benefits. Thus, decisions to inform others should be determined within the context of the therapeutic setting, and the benefits and costs associated with disclosing such information should be carefully evaluated.

Another option for intervention is known as "coaching." The term denotes a specific relationship between a healthcare professional or paraprofessional and a person with ADHD, usually an adolescent or adult. Successful coaching relationships are contingent on the competence of the coach, the motivation of the individual with ADHD, and the interpersonal fit between them (Brown, 2000). Coaching usually involves the identification of problem symptoms or behaviors, and the development and monitoring of concrete plans that address the functioning and progress of the individual with ADHD. Although such objectives are usually features of any psychotherapeutic interventions, the coaching relationship differs slightly in that it particularly emphasizes these goals and behaviors, and may attend less to the emotional effects of the disorder. Coaching relationships are also distinguished by frequent communications, usually by phone, between the coach and the individual with ADHD (Brown, 2000). Murphy (2005) explains that coaching differs from traditional psychotherapy, since psychotherapy usually involves the identification of specific goals, whereas coaching consists of turning these goals into strategies and actions.

Some individuals with ADHD, or parents of children with ADHD, may find it helpful to join self-help or support groups. Children and Adults with Attention-Deficit Disorder (CHADD) and the National Attention Deficit Disorder Association both provide information, support, and resources for individuals and families affected by ADHD. These groups are often helpful in providing current information about ADHD, and also offer the benefits of a support network that may assist individuals to cope with the disorder and become effective advocates for themselves or their family members.

### 4.1.5    Interventions with Teachers and Schools

**It is important that parents and teachers are aware of the Individuals with Disabilities Education Act and Section 504 of the Rehabilitation Act of 1976**

It is important that families and teachers are aware of the federal mandates that ensure the rights of children with ADHD in the United States who demonstrate eligibility under recent legislation. These include the Individuals with Disabilities Education Act (IDEA) and Section 504 of the Rehabilitation Act of 1973 (Section 504). School districts are required to offer "free appropriate public education" to eligible children who qualify for these services because they have a specific disability. Many children with ADHD may not meet criteria for services under IDEA, but may be protected under Section 504.

Individuals whose ADHD does not affect their learning processes may not be considered eligible for services under IDEA or Section 504.

Under IDEA, ADHD may be viewed as pertaining to the category of "Other Health Impairment" (OHI), if the disorder manifests itself through impairments in vitality, strength, or alertness. The IDEA requires every school district to obtain a complete evaluation for each child who may be eligible for special education and related programs. After the evaluation, the child's Individualized Education Program (IEP) team considers the evaluation for the purpose of creating a plan that addresses the educational needs of the child. An ADHD diagnosis in and of itself does not necessarily indicate that a child is eligible for special education services or other programs. Children with ADHD also may meet requirements under other disability categories of IDEA, such as "Specific Learning Disability," or "Emotional Disturbance," if the individuals have comorbid diagnoses (e.g., ADHD and a psychiatric diagnosis; ADHD and a learning disability).

If a child is eligible for services under IDEA, teachers, mental health professionals, and parents create an IEP plan that includes specific goals that are assessed each year. These goals may include standards for academic achievement, emotional functioning, and specific behavioral objectives. Parents participate in developing the IEP, and the plan cannot be changed without their input. Every child who receives services through IDEA must have an IEP.

Students with ADHD who obtain services through Section 504 are provided with programs created to address their specific challenges and needs. Children who are deemed eligible for Section 504 must demonstrate that the disorder requires special programs or educational formats. Such modifications may consist of curriculum changes, different classroom organizations, tailored teaching techniques and instructions for homework and studying, behavior management techniques, and increased dialogue between parents and teachers.

Managing children with ADHD is often challenging for teachers and schools. ADHD symptoms can affect attention, comprehension, assignment completion, and group dynamics within the classroom setting. The frustration students experience as a result of ADHD may be associated with additional behavior problems such as aggression, emotional lability, or tantrums. Teachers may benefit from introducing the most difficult material at the beginning of the day, by clarifying the steps needed to complete tasks, by minimizing multitasking requirements, by varying methods of instruction, and by alleviating potentially distracting elements from the students' environments. Teachers can also maximize the effectiveness of interactions with students with ADHD by giving clear and concise instructions, maintaining eye contact with the student, remaining calm, and by establishing and following clear and consistent classroom rules. Teachers should endeavor to respond with sensitivity and cultivate self-esteem in individuals with ADHD. Rewards are likely to be more effective than punishments, and teachers can assist in identifying methods of encouraging each student in negotiating many of the challenges associated with ADHD.

Though social and cultural forces operating within some families and societies may place a strong emphasis on obtaining a college degree as a prerequisite for success, this ideal may not be appropriate for some individuals with ADHD, and may even constitute an obstacle (Murphy, 2005). College students have many distractions that can exacerbate difficulties with concentration and result in failure. Mainstream college education may suit high-functioning adolescents and young adults with ADHD who have already developed effective compensatory strategies or interventions, but other individuals may find various alternatives to traditional four-year colleges acceptable or even preferable. Such alternatives may include junior colleges, internships, trade schools, work, or service programs (Murphy, 2005). It also should be noted that most colleges and universities provide services for students with special learning needs, including those with ADHD and learning disabilities.

### 4.1.6    Social Skills Training

Social skills training may be useful for children who have ADHD, although research has not always demonstrated its efficacy. Inattention and hyperactivity can preclude children from forming appropriate relationships with their peers, learning to listen, taking turns, and controlling impulses that can facilitate the development of healthy friendships. Research indicates that individuals with ADHD exhibit significantly more problems with peer relationships when compared to those without the disorder, but also suggests that a heavy focus on social skills deficits may improve social functioning (Gol & Jarus, 2005) and hopefully peer relationships as well.

**Computer programs can be used to successfully train working memory**

Cognitive training utilizing computers is a new treatment for ADHD. Developed by a neuroscientist named Klingberg, the training targets working memory, a domain that may not be improved by the use of stimulant medications. The intervention takes the form of a software program that children use over the course of several weeks (Sinha, 2004). Klingberg, Fernell, Olesen, Johnson, Gustafsson, Dahlstrom et al. (2005) conducted a randomized double-blind, controlled investigation of a computer program to train working memory. Among the 44 children with ADHD who completed the training there were significant improvements in working memory. Parents also reported reduced levels of inattention and hyperactivity/impulsivity. These ratings endured at three month follow-up.

### 4.2    Mechanisms of Action

The stimulants produce their effects through the neurotransmitters, the various chemicals through which the brain's neurons communicate with each other. Specifically, it is hypothesized that the stimulants increase dopamine and norepinephrine activity at the synaptic level of the central nervous system (CNS). Stimulant medication increases neurotransmitter activity, which in turn enhances attention and concentration.

Psychotherapy is likely to effect change in a multitude of ways. For adults, when therapists respect the experiences of their patients and communicate understanding and empathy, they may change patients' understanding about relationships and their sense of self. In addition, structured forms of psychotherapy for some older children and adolescents as well as adults may assist persons with ADHD in forming goals, identifying obstacles, and meeting challenges in ways that can be applied to everyday situations. Finally, psychoeducational components of therapy for ADHD can enable patients and families to gain a better understanding of ADHD, and enable them to make more informed treatment decisions.

Behavior therapy offers patients specific tools and behaviors through which they can address the difficulties they experience that are related to ADHD. When therapists and patients agree on strategies to incorporate in order to cope with the disorder, these may be practiced both within and outside of therapy sessions. Such strategies may include list-making, creating specific times set aside for organizational tasks, and assessments of plans and priorities. If the chosen coping mechanisms prove effective, patients may learn new methods that can replace old patterns and habits. The same principles are relevant for parents of children with ADHD or for adults with ADHD whose parenting is affected by the disorder. Learning new and effective parenting techniques demands an initial investment of time and practice; however, new methods are eventually learned, and can become automatic, consistent, and effective responses that deter undesirable behaviors and promote positive actions.

## 4.2.1 Alternative Treatments

Reiff & Tippins (2004) believe a variety of ADHD symptoms and disorders may be managed through diet. They affirm that research has demonstrated that individuals' moods and behaviors are indeed affected by diet. Perhaps both this cultural emphasis on diet, and such data regarding connections between diet and emotional functioning, bolstered the popularity of dietary interventions for ADHD. For example, many people are concerned about the sugar content, artificial ingredients, and other additives that are ubiquitous in the typical American diet. Finally, it is possible that food allergies and sensitivities, as well as negative reactions to other environmental substances, do affect children's behavior and health.

> **It is believed that many ADHD symptoms can be managed through diet**

During the 1970s, and 1980s Feingold (e.g., 1985) claimed that 50% of children with hyperactivity could be cured by adopting a diet free of food additives. Feingold was an allergist who believed that food additives, including dyes and artificial flavorings as well as salicylates, which are contained in many vegetables and fruits, were responsible for learning disorders and hyperactivity in children (Rieff & Tippins, 2004). Feingold asserted that diets that eliminated these substances elicited considerable improvements in over half of children with these symptoms.

The Feingold diet became immensely popular in the United States, and led to the creation of the Feingold Association of the United States. However, the diet was based on anecdotal descriptions rather than scientific data. After considerable public acceptance of the diet, scientists began to investigate the effects of the Feingold diet (Weiss et al., 1999). Findings provide little support for the Feingold diet, and it does not appear to affect either the symptoms associated with ADHD or the functional impairments exhibited by these individuals.

The interest in food additives followed earlier ideas that megavitamins could help children with ADHD (Weiss et al., 1999). Other individuals have suggested that sugar either causes ADHD or exacerbates the effects of the disorder. However, research does not support this hypothesis (e.g., Wolraich, Lindgren, Stumbo, Steglink, Appelbaum, & Kiritsy, 1994; Behar, Rapoport, Adams, Berg, & Cornblath, 1989).

**Hunger and malnutrition can affect concentration and impulsivity**

Weiss et al. (1999) bring up the interesting observation that despite public fascination with the ways that eating habits may influence the development or course of ADHD, there has been little attention focused on the potential ways that the serious hunger and malnutrition faced by many children may affect their thinking and behavior. Poverty causes many children to come to school very hungry, and these students often don't have the money necessary to purchase lunch. States of extreme hunger are likely to affect students' levels of concentration and impulsivity (Weiss et al., 1999).

**Many dietary supplements and herbs are marketed for ADHD treatment There is no available evidence to support the efficacy of these treatment for ADHD and they should be used with care**

Proponents of popular approaches to treating ADHD have promoted other dietary supplements, including antioxidants, nootropics ("smart drugs"), and herbs. Other over-the-counter ADHD remedies include deanol (DMAE), lecithin, and phosphatylserine (Rieff & Tippins, 2004). Other substances that have been advertised as treatments for ADHD are melatonin (an antioxidant used to ameliorate difficulties with sleep cycles), pycnogenol (an antioxidant gathered from pine bark), and gingko biloba (commonly used in Europe to treat circulatory and memory disorders). There are also herbs marketed for ADHD such as chamomile, valerian, lemon balm, hops, passion flower, and kava.

Many other treatments that have been suggested for ADHD, which include massage, meditation, vestibular stimulation, iron supplementation, magnesium supplementation, Chinese herbals, EEG biofeedback, mirror feedback, and channel-specific perceptual training. Though some of these are supported by prospective pilot data, others are not well-researched (Arnold, 2001).

It is extremely important that patients, or the parents of children, notify their physicians when attempting to use alternative remedies in addition to allopathic ones. It is possible that some alternative substances may harm individuals when those substances are combined with other treatments. For instance, gingko biloba is dangerous when combined with aspirin, antidepressants, or anticoagulants, and other herbs may be harmful when combined with sedative medications through compound effects (Rieff & Tippins 2004). There is clearly no available evidence for the efficacy of alternative therapies in the management of ADHD, and given the potential deleterious effects of these agents either alone in combination with other medications, these agents should be used with extreme caution if at all.

## 4.3    Efficacy and Prognosis

**Stimulant medication effectively decreases ADHD symptoms, but little is known about the long-term effects**

There are many research studies that indicate stimulant medications decrease ADHD symptoms and difficulties, at least in the short-term. It is important to note, however, that most clinical trials examining the efficacy of stimulant medications have been conducted only over very short periods of time, and in homogenous samples that most often consist of Caucasian boys (Wilens et al., 2000b). There are a few long-term follow-up studies that have investigated the effects of stimulant medication. Charach, Ickowicz, and Schachar (2004) examined the effects of stimulant medication over five years for 79 children diagnosed with ADHD, and found that both benefits and side effects endured over the period of the study while the children were on active medication. Double-blind clinical trials that include placebo controls have documented that stimulants are more effective than placebo for enhancing attention and concentration, and for diminishing hyperactivity and impulsivity for children with ADHD (Brown & La Rosa, 2002).

Research has demonstrated that stimulant medications significantly improve cognitive performance on a multitude of tasks related to short-term memory, vigilance, reaction time, and learning of both verbal and nonverbal information. Other domains that are enhanced by stimulant medication include distractibility, inhibitory control, and perceptual-motor function. For instance, methylphenidate enhances cognitive performance among children with ADHD (Kempton, Vance, Maruff, Luk, Costin, & Pantelis, 1999; Riordan, Flashman, Saykin, Frutiger, Carroll, & Huey, 1999). Children taking methylphenidate also exhibit higher ratings of academic efficiency, productivity, and attention (DuPaul & Rapport, 1993), and reduced impulsive responding on cognitive tasks (Tannock, Schachar, & Logan, 1995). Although stimulants improve short-term academic achievement in children, long-term benefits on academic achievement have yet to be demonstrated (Bennett, Brown, Craver, & Anderson, 1999). Brown, Dreelin, and Dingle (1997) suggest that stimulant medications primarily affect academic productivity and efficiency, rather than the types of achievement measured by tests or standardized instruments. In general, psychostimulants produce beneficial effects on measures of cognitive tasks that are related to executive functions (for a review, see Brown & Sammons, 2003).

Stimulants also appear to influence relationships. Barkley (1998b) reported that stimulants contribute to improvements in interactions among parents and children, and among children and their siblings. They also appear to reduce antisocial behaviors including conduct problems, negative verbalizations, and physical aggression (Hinshsaw, 1991; Pelham, Aronoff, Midlam, Shapiro, Gnagy, Chronis et al., 1999). It is important to note, however, that some studies reported nonsignificant results for the effects of stimulants on aggressive behaviors (e.g., Hinshaw, Henker, & Whalen, 1984; Matier, Halperin, Sharma, Newcorn, & Sathaye 1992). Stimulants have been shown to improve social interactions (Wilens & Spencer, 2000), peer relationships (Brown & Sawyer, 1998), communication, and responsiveness (Hinshaw, Heller, & McHale, 1992). Although stimulants are related to improved social functioning in children, they seldom normalize the behavior of children with ADHD to that of their peers without the disorder (Pfiffner, Calzada, & McBurnett, 2000).

Stimulants seem to help children with compliance with classroom rules (Barkley, 1990; Carlson et al., 1992). Not all findings, however, provide consistent results. For instance, some research has suggested that methylphenidate improves classroom behavior as rated by teachers, but these effects do not mirror behavioral improvements as observed by parents (Bukstein & Kolko, 1998; Schachar, Tannock, Cunningham, & Corkum, 1997).

In a double-blind study that examined the efficacy of methylphenidate and dextroamphetamine for children (Efron, Jarman, & Baker, 1997), the two stimulants each resulted in significant improvements from baseline assessments across all measures. Jadad, Booker, Gauld, Kakuma, Boyle, Cummingham et al. (1999) examined 22 studies, and determined that there were no differences between methylphenidate and dextroamphetamine in managing the core symptoms associated with ADHD. It is interesting to note that stimulant medication alleviates functional impairments beyond the specific symptoms that these medications target. Barkley et al. (2005) provide data to indicate that medicated adults and adolescents with ADHD may be at significantly lower risk for automobile accidents than nonmedicated individuals with ADHD.

There are few differences across medications with regards to side effects. Efron et al. (1997) did report higher insomnia ratings for patients on dextroamphetamine as compared with patients on methylphenidate, but noted that appetite disturbances were rated similarly for the two medications. Another study (Grcevich, Rowane, & Marcellino, 2001) contrasted methylphenidate and Adderall, and found no differences in adverse effects. Patients often experience rebound effects (increased overactivity or inattention from baseline levels when a drug wears off) when they cease taking medication.

Up to 30% of children, and as many as 50% of adults do not respond to stimulant medications for ADHD (Brown, 2000). There do not appear to be any behavioral or diagnostic predictors that might help individuals, families, and clinicians determine whether someone with ADHD will respond to stimulant medication. Often individuals who do not experience a decrease in ADHD symptoms after receiving one stimulant medication may respond well to another, although there are some who simply do not experience the alleviation of symptoms under any stimulant medication.

**Tricyclic antidepressants have been shown to be effective in treating ADHD**

There also are studies demonstrating the efficacy of tricyclic antidepressants for ADHD. In a clinical sample of 62 children and adolescents treated with desipramine, Biederman, Baldessarini, Wright, Knee, and Harmatz (1989) found significant clinical and behavioral improvements. Wilens, Biederman, Prince, Spencer, Faraone, Warburton et al. (1996) found that desipramine was also beneficial in a controlled clinical trial that included 41 adults with ADHD. Research indicates that modafinil (Provigil) is effective in reducing ADHD symptoms in both children (e.g., Biederman, Swanson, Wigal, Kratochvil, Boellner, Earl et al., 2005) and adults (Turner, Clark, Dowson, Robbins, & Sahakian, 2004).

Owens, Hinshaw, Kraemer, Arnold, & Abikoff (2003) used data from the MTA study to identify variables that would predict response to ADHD treatment for children. Although the investigators did not indicate any reliable predictors, the findings did identify some variables that moderate responses to treatment. These variables included parental symptoms of depression, severity of ADHD symptoms, and children's intellectual functioning.

Pisterman et al. (1989) report several benefits from a training program for preschoolers with ADHD and their parents. After the training program with their parents, preschoolers were more compliant. Further, parents' treatment of their children was more consistent and directive, and parents demonstrated increased positive reinforcement for compliant behaviors. Bor, Sanders, and Markie-Dadds (2002) developed a parent intervention program designed to improve disruptive behaviors and ADHD symptoms among preschoolers. The intervention resulted in improved parenting skills and competence as well as a reduction in the behavior problems that parents reported in direct observations of their children.

There is minimal research to substantiate the efficacy of social skills training. Antschel and Remer (2003) found that among 120 children with ADHD who received eight weeks of social skills training, the intervention improved their self-reports of assertiveness, although the social skills training did not generalize to other social functions.

Wilens, McDermott, Biederman, Abrantes, Hakesy, & Spencer (1999) report significant benefits for adults with ADHD treated with cognitive therapy. Hesslinger, Tebartz van Elst, Nyber, Dykierek, Richter, Berner, and Ebert (2002) describe a group intervention for adults with ADHD that included psychoeducation and instruction in cognitive behavioral and dialectical behavioral techniques. The intervention targeted emotional regulation, controlling impulsivity, and aspects of interactions between ADHD and interpersonal and intrapersonal functions. Treatment resulted in reduced levels of symptoms associated with ADHD and depressive symptoms. This therapy does not appear to be as effective with children. Research examining cognitive approaches for children and adolescents with ADHD has not found cognitive therapy to be especially useful with these age groups due to the lack of generalizability or durability (for a review, see Gittelman & Abikoff, 1989).

**Cognitive therapy has been found to be effective in adults with ADHD, but does not appear effective in children and adolescents**

There is currently research in progress addressing the efficacy of coaching for ADHD. Brown (2000) describes anecdotal reports of satisfactory results from coaching interventions. There are other clinical reports provided by clients who had high expectations regarding coaching, but who were ultimately disappointed by the outcome of this intervention. Clearly, future research efforts are necessary to determine whether coaching interventions do in fact provide meaningful benefits.

In a randomized, controlled trial, cognitive training for ADHD through the use of software programs significantly improved ADHD symptoms in children (Klingberg et al., 2005). Though the computer program targets working memory, parents reported improvements in inattention and hyperactivity following the training program. More research is necessary to determine if such a training program should be incorporated into treatments with children and potentially adults with ADHD.

Alternative remedies for ADHD are still being researched. Despite the initial popularity of the Feingold diet, controlled research studies indicate that only about 10% of children with ADHD demonstrated allergies to food dyes, and only 2% responded to the elimination of food dyes with behavioral improvements (Rieff & Tippins, 2004). Studies investigating the Feingold diet generally compared two diets that seemed identical. Participants were not aware if they were in the condition with or without food additives. Conners (1980) analyzed the results of these studies, and determined that with the exception of a small minority of preschool children, there were no significant differences resulting from diets with or without food additives.

Other alternative remedies for ADHD are also being researched, with some encouraging results (Arnold, 2001). Though one promising study indicated that dimethylethanolamine (deanol; DMAE) may be as helpful as methylphenidate in improving target behaviors, more research is necessary. Many individuals anecdotally report beneficial effects from herbs and alternative remedies; controlled studies, however, are required to elucidate their efficacy (Rieff & Tippings, 2004).

# 4.4     Variations and Combinations of Methods

Combining psychotropic medications with psychological interventions is often the preferred way to manage ADHD symptoms. For example, Safren, Otto, Sprich, Winett, Wilens, & Biederman (2005) used cognitive-behavior therapy to produce reductions in ADHD symptoms and anxiety related symptoms among adults that were greater than those obtained by medication alone. For pediatric populations, however, some studies have not provided compelling data to suggest the benefits of combined treatments of pharmacotherapy and psychotherapy relative to medication alone. For example, in a sample of 103 children with ADHD ranging in age from seven to nine years who received social skills training and methylphenidate, Abikoff, Hechtman, Klein, Gallagher, Fleiss, Etcovitch et al., (2004) did not find social skills intervention to be particularly efficacious; nor were there benefits from the combined treatment of social skills training and methylphenidate in emotional or academic functioning (Hechtman, Abikoff, Klein, Weiss, Respitz, Kouri et al., 2004). It does appear, however, that combining medication with psychosocial treatment is more effective when the intervention also includes parent training. Tutty, Gephart and Wurzbacher (2003) evaluated an intervention in 100 children with ADHD ranging in age from 5 to 12 years who received stimulant medication and their parents. The intervention program provided eight weeks of behavioral and social skills instruction. Following the intervention, the parents in the group reported fewer ADHD symptoms in their children and improved parenting practices as compared with a control group who did not receive the intervention.

**Stimulant medication effectively decreases ADHD symptoms, but little is known about the long-term effects**

An NIMH study entitled the Multimodal Treatment Study of Children with ADHD (MTA) presents comprehensive data regarding the efficacy of combined treatments for ADHD (MTA Cooperative Group, 1999a, 1999b). The study collected longitudinal data from 579 children between the ages seven to ten years at six university medical centers in the United States and Canada. The investigation compared the effects of four interventions, which included a behavioral intervention alone, psychotropic medication supplied by the researchers, a combination of medication and a behavioral intervention, and a control condition of routine community care without an intervention.

Findings revealed that behavioral treatments and medication are superior to behavioral approaches alone or typical community care for children with ADHD and comorbid anxiety disorders. Benefits were observed over a period of 14 months. Multimodal treatment was also most effective in mitigating related areas of functional impairments, including troubled family relationships, social skills deficits, defiant and oppositional behavior, as well as poor academic achievement.

Based on their data, the MTA investigators recommended that multimodal treatments are strongly indicated for children who are encountering specific environmental stressors, and for children who evidence comorbid depression or anxiety in addition to ADHD. (It is especially noteworthy that children who received combined treatment modalities required lower stimulant dosages than those who were treated with medication alone).

Reports also suggest that school behavior and parenting skills also improve in response to multimodal treatment (Hinshaw, Owens, Wells, & Abikoff, 2000).

The study's results were consistent across all six research sites, even though participant demographic characteristics were heterogeneous. Multimodal treatments may be especially helpful for children who do not respond to medication alone (Klein, Abikoff, Klass, Ganeles, Seese, & Pollack, 1997). Students may also have co-occurring problems such as learning problems or affective disorders that may pose additional problems for teachers.

## 4.4.1    Comorbid Conditions

Spencer et al. (2000) note that there are few controlled clinical trials that have examined pharmacologic interventions for children and adolescents who have comorbid mood disorders and ADHD. Physicians who prescribe medications for depressive disorders typically select medications from four classes of psychotropic agents: tricyclic antidepressants (TCAs), monoamine oxidase inhibitors (MAOIs), selective serotonin reuptake inhibitors (SSRIs), and atypical antidepressants (e.g., bupropion). Bipolar disorders are usually treated with mood stabilizing medications, including lithium or anticonvulsants. Children with comorbid mood disorders may be less likely to respond to stimulant treatment for ADHD (DuPaul, Barkley, & McMurray, 1994). These findings are important as they underscore the importance of subtyping according to comorbidity in predicting response to stimulant medications.

**Children with comorbid mood disorders are less likely to respond to stimulant medication**

Although many individuals may consider ADHD to be a less serious condition than depression, Spencer et al., (2000) point out that ADHD can impair individuals' academic, occupational, and social functioning. These impairments may prevent individuals from enjoying success in these important areas of life, and may contribute to their depressive symptoms. Spencer et al. have recommended a treatment program that includes stimulants and antidepressant medications. They identify the classes of antidepressants that may target both conditions effectively. These include TCAs, MAOIs, and atypical antidepressants, including buproprion. There is some evidence that individuals with both mania and ADHD may not respond well to lithium (e.g., McElroy, Keck, Pope, Hudson, Faedda, & Swann, 1992).

Two clinical trials (Findling, 1996; Gammon & Brown, 1993) reported beneficial results from combined stimulant and SSRI pharmacologic interventions in individuals with comorbid depression and ADHD. In an investigation that evaluated the effects of desipramine on children and adolescents with ADHD, Biederman, Baldessarini, Wright, Keenan, and Faraone (1993) determined that there were no differences in response for children who had comorbid depression, anxiety, or conduct disorders and those who had ADHD alone. Spencer, Wilens, Biederman, Faraone, Ablon, and Lapey (1995) noted positive responses to methylphenidate in adults with ADHD, and observed that these effects were independent of lifetime depression or family psychiatric histories. Individuals with ADHD and depressive symptoms are likely to benefit from psychotherapy that addresses all of their depressive symptoms, including those that interact or result from ADHD.

Tannock and Brown (2000) notes that many parents and teachers may observe the behavioral symptoms that comprise one element of ADHD, but may be unaware of children's symptoms associated with anxiety. It is therefore necessary to provide psychoeducation to parents and teachers that addresses the possibility of anxiety-related symptoms, such as worry or fear. These concerns may be more salient to these children's overall functioning than difficulties with attention and hyperactivity. For this reason treatment plans should determine appropriate methods to address anxiety symptoms in each patient as well as symptoms associated with ADHD. Tannock and Brown (2000) has recommended that children, teachers, and parents each should take part in determining which symptoms should be initially targeted, and subsequently evaluate whether the treatment is assisting in resolving symptoms that are particularly problematic and impairing functioning.

**Antidepressants are often recommended for adults and adolescents with substance use disorders because of the addictive potential of stimulant medication**

When individuals with ADHD also have substance use disorders, health care professionals should attend to both disorders, but need to initially prioritize treatment of the substance use disorder (Wilens et al., 2000a). If the substance use disorder is very serious, patients may need hospitalization in an inpatient facility. Eventually, treatment should address both disorders and the ways that they may interact. The trajectory of the disorders is likely to influence prognoses. Each disorder may exacerbate the other (Wilens et al., 2000a). ADHD clearly seems to increase the risk for the development of substance use disorders. When children with ADHD are treated with psychostimulant medication, they are less likely than untreated children to have alcohol or drug disorders later in life (Wilens, Faraone, Biederman, & Gunawardene, 2003). Antidepressants such as buprorion or tricyclics are often recommended for adolescents or adults with comorbid ADHD and substance use disorders (e.g., Sohkhah, Wilens, Daly, Prince, Van Patten, & Biedermanet, 2005; Riggs, 1998), given the addictive potential of the stimulants. Both antidepressant and stimulant medication, however, appear to lessen substance use or cravings (e.g., Riggs, et al., 1996). For example, among adults with ADHD and cocaine addiction, Levin, Evans, & Kleber (1999) found that methylphenidate diminished significantly cravings for cocaine.

Current research does not suggest any association between stimulant medication use and an increased propensity for substance use disorders. However, those prescribing stimulant medications should be judicious, particularly when prescribing the medication for adolescents and adults and for children when there is a substance-abusing parent or sibling at home. The astute practitioner must be mindful of the fact that the stimulants are often used for recreational or academic purposes among individuals who do not have ADHD. For example, in one study of college students, Hall, Irwin, Bowman, Frankenberger, and Jewett (2005) reported that 11% of 202 university women and 17% of 179 university men indicated via questionnaires that they had illegally used stimulants that had been prescribed for others. Wilens et al. (2000a) note that there is less likelihood that methylphenidate will be abused than will the amphetamines or methamphetamine.

Responses to treatment for individuals with ADHD and comorbid disorders may differentially affect cognitive, behavioral, and emotional functioning. Providers should consider a combination of treatment types, including behavioral and cognitive-behavioral interventions, psychoeducation, and pharmacologic interventions. Tannock and Brown (2000) advise practitioners to begin pharmacotherapy by evaluating whether individuals respond to a single drug, such as methylphenidate or an antidepressant, before attempting to prescribe multiple medications. Since methylphenidate may not prove beneficial for many individuals, Tannock and Brown (2000) suggest trying another stimulant, such as dextroamphetamine, prior to changing classes of medication such as antidepressants (e.g., a tricyclic) or other drugs. Data from the MTA study indicate that children with ADHD and comorbid anxiety disorders (but not ODD or CD) responded both to stimulant medication and behavioral therapy as well as individuals with ADD alone (Jensen et al., 2001). Newcorn and Halperin (2000) have noted that there is a dearth of empirical research regarding effective pharmacologic and psychosocial treatments for children with ADHD who also exhibit oppositional behavior and aggression. Clearly, additional clinical trials are needed in this area.

Comings (2000) recommends clonidine for the management of comorbid ADHD and tics, and reports that prescribing both stimulant medication and clonidine can be beneficial for this population. In addition, the tricyclic antidepressants such as imipramine and desipramine may be helpful for children with ADHD who have comorbid Tourette's disorder. These antidepressants do not pose risks of precipitating or exacerbating Tourette's disorder, unlike stimulants that can trigger or worsen tics in individuals with ADHD and Tourette's syndrome (Robertson & Eapen, 1992). However, it should be noted that other studies have suggested that higher doses of methylphenidate may reduce tics (Gadow, Nolan, & Sverd, 1992), although much more research is needed prior to routine administration of methylphenidate for individuals with Tourette's.

Brown (2000) notes that most investigations of pharmacologic treatments for children with obsessive-compulsive disorder have demonstrated the effectiveness of the selective serotonin reuptake inhibitors (SSRIs), although the SSRIs have not been shown to produce benefits for cognitive impairments associated with ADHD. Conversely, the stimulant medications that have demonstrated the most improvements for the cognitive impairments associated with ADHD are not particularly helpful in treating OCD. Though combining SSRIs and stimulant treatment for the purpose of targeting both ADHD and OCD symptoms may at first examination appear to be appropriate, there are no controlled studies that have evaluated this combination of medications for individuals affected by both OCD and ADHD. Prior to engaging in polypharmacy (use of multiple medications), much more research needs to be available examining the efficacy of combinations of medication.

Stimulant medication may not be beneficial for children with ADHD and comorbid anxiety disorders (Tannock & Brown, 2000). Research regarding specific domains related to ADHD underscores the attenuation of pharmacologic benefits for children with concurrent anxiety. For example, one study indicates that methylphenidate increased working memory performance for children with ADHD without anxiety disorders, but that it did not ameliorate working memory for children with both ADHD and an anxiety disorder. Since anxiety can exacerbate the cognitive difficulties experienced by individuals with ADHD, finding appropriate interventions are especially important for those affected by both disorders.

Children with both ADHD and anxiety disorders may experience more adverse side effects from stimulant medications (Ickowicz, Tannock, Fulford Purvis, & Schachar, 1992). However, the literature has been equivocal with regard to the use of stimulants for those with ADHD and comorbid anxiety disorders. For example, some studies have not demonstrated differences in behavioral responses or adverse side effects following stimulant treatment for individuals with ADHD alone and those with comorbid ADHD and anxiety disorders (e.g., Diamond, Tannock, & Schachar, 1999). Tannock and Brown (2000) state that because of its physical properties, clonidine may be helpful for individuals with comorbid anxiety disorders and ADHD, but cautions that there are no controlled trials that have systematically examined clonidine in this patient population. Tannock notes that there is no research to demonstrate that any one type of medication targets the spectrum of behavioral and emotional symptoms of individuals who have both ADHD and an anxiety disorder. Hence, a combination of pharmacotherapy and psychotherapy seems to be the most appropriate treatment choice at this point in time.

Individuals with comorbid ADHD and learning disorders are best treated with a comprehensive approach and several therapies, including potentially psychotropic medication and psychoeducational treatments. For children, this will involve an IEP that will implement accommodations and strategies that target both disorders. Medication is commonly used in children with ADHD and comorbid learning disorders. Stimulant medication has been shown to increase academic productivity (e.g., Elia, Welsh, Gullotta, &Rapoport, 1993; Pelham, 1993). However, the mechanisms through which stimulant medications may target the cognitive processes thought to underlie learning disorders are unclear. Stimulants may increase computational productivity, information retrieval, or word recognition. It seems that stimulant medications provide a generalized enhancement of cognitive processing (Tannock & Brown, 2000), although their specific effects on academic achievement have yet to be demonstrated. Tannock and Brown caution that even when stimulant treatment is successful for individuals who have both ADHD and learning disorders, it is usually insufficient. For children with both ADHD and learning disorders, in-school modifications should be supplemented with interventions outside of school. Such interventions may include audio or videotaped books or lessons, computer instruction, parent tutoring, supervision for studying, assignment completion, and organization, and counseling. Training with computers may be especially beneficial for individuals with learning disorders, especially for those who have challenges expressing themselves verbally. When children have early and comprehensive instruction in keyboard skills and software usage, these skills can become ingrained and serve as valuable tools throughout children's education and future employment. Audio or video presentations may help students with difficulties in reading gain a better sense of their written work. Murphy (2005) further recommends personal digital assistants (PDAs) that can include daily planners, to-do lists, and alerts for reminders of different tasks and activities. Though research does not exist to verify the importance of these interventions, therapists have described the meaningful benefits that such practices elicit in their patients (Tannock & Brown, 2000).

Students who have comorbid learning disorders and ADHD often face difficulties with self-esteem and serious stress that result from their challenges in meeting academic demands. They may experience conflicts with parents, teachers, or peers who do not understand these conditions. Often, this stress escalates during the high school years as adolescents begin to plan for the future. Parents may experience this stress as well, and they may help or exacerbate students' difficulties with homework, studying, and organization. Students and parents may benefit from discussing their concerns with a counselor or advisor who understands these conditions and may offer support and guidance. Often, psychotherapy is useful in order to address the interpersonal and intrapersonal issues that arise in response to these disorders, and may help students and parents develop reasonable expectations and coping methods (Tannock & Brown, 2000).

When children or adolescents are identified as having comorbid ADHD and oppositional defiant disorder or conduct disorder, a comprehensive treatment approach is often needed. Mannuzza et al. (1993) found that when ADHD symptoms persist into adolescence or adulthood, they constitute the most serious risk factor for the development of conduct disorder. In addition, children with ADHD who evidence traits of antisocial personalities have increased risk for substance use. For these reasons, it is especially important to employ early interventions for children affected by ADHD who demonstrate antisocial behaviors (Newcorn & Halperin, 2000). Since therapists may fail to observe signs of ADHD among youth who have OCD or CD, especially in girls who may express fewer visible symptoms, a thorough assessment is necessary.

Children who have both conditions may respond well to stimulant medication or antidepressants. Psychosocial treatments may target aspects of impulsivity that relate to both disorders and can provide helpful behavioral goals and alternatives. Many children with these conditions have both externalizing and internalizing problems; therefore, therapists should attempt to ensure that treatment addresses a range of possible symptoms (Newcorn & Halperin, 2000).

Stimulant treatment with methylphenidate appears to be efficacious for children with ADHD and comorbid aggression (Barkley, 1989; Klorman, Brumaghim, Salzman, Strauss, Borgstedt, McBride, & Loeb, 1998), in a similar manner for children who have ADHD alone. In addition, stimulant medication may reduce aggressive behaviors (e.g., Kaplan, Busner, Kupietz, Wassermann, & Segal, 1990). There is some research to suggest that children with ADHD and ODD may benefit from a combination of fluoxetine (Prozac) and methylphenidate (Gammon & Brown, 1993). Other research (Constantino, Liberman, & Kincaid, 1997), however, has suggested that the SSRIs may exacerbate difficult behaviors in children with aggression. Although researchers have examined the effects of lithium on children's aggression, there are no data to support the efficacy of this pharmacotherapy for comorbid ADHD and aggression (Newcorn & Halperin, 2000). Similarly, there is little research that has specifically addressed the efficacy of therapeutic treatments for children with both conditions. Treatment typically involves parent training, daily observations and self-monitoring, and cognitive behavioral techniques.

## 4.5 Problems in Carrying out the Treatments

Although many individuals benefit from stimulant medication, frequently there are adverse side effects associated with the use of stimulants. Individuals may describe nervousness, insomnia, loss of appetite or weight, and headaches. In

**Stimulant medication may interfere with the healthy growth of children, so their weight and height should be monitored carefully when taking the medication**

children, there has been some evidence that the stimulants may interfere with healthy growth; therefore, children's height and weight should be monitored when being managed with stimulant medications. Some patients report experiencing irritability or depression as the effects of the drug begin to wane. Research generally has revealed that different informants may provide distinct information regarding the adverse side effects of those with the disorder, with parents generally providing the most useful information (DuPaul, 1991).

Specific medications for ADHD carry potential health risks. Since pemoline is associated with hepatic failure, it is no longer recommended as a viable treatment for ADHD. Although Adderall was taken off of the market for several months in 2005 in Canada following isolated reports of strokes and deaths in those taking the medication, it was returned to the market because of the lack of any compelling evidence that it was dangerous or that it was associated with any more adverse side effects than any other stimulant medication. Stimulant medication should be prescribed for children under the age of six years of age with great care, since the long-term effects for this age group have not been established. Moreover, children under the age of six years are likely to experience a greater frequency of adverse side effects than their older counterparts. Barkley (1990) advises against prescribing stimulants to children under four, since efficacy for these drugs decreases for children younger than five years of age, and because the drugs target the prefrontal cortex, which is not fully developed in children under five years old. Furthermore, the physiological systems responsible for metabolizing and secreting stimulants are also undeveloped at that age (Barkley, 1989). Stimulants also should be used with utmost caution in women of childbearing age because of the potential deleterious effects to the fetus in women who are pregnant.

Atomoxetine (Strattera) has many potential adverse side effects, including vomiting, gastrointestinal disturbances, dizziness, headaches, mood swings, weight loss, sexual dysfunction, violent behavior, irritability, fatigue, constipation, painful menstruation, fever, chills, hot flashes, sweating, and muscle pain (National Institute of Health, 2005). In addition, some studies have reported an association between administration of atomoxetine and an increased risk of suicide. Manufacturers of the drug now identify this risk on the label, and this potential risk should be taken into consideration by those prescribing medications for individuals with ADHD.

Individuals who receive tricyclic antidepressants (TCAs) may experience several adverse side effects, including fatigue, weight gain, constipation, dry mouth, and sexual dysfunction.

There have been reports of sudden death in children treated with desipramine (e.g., Biederman, et al., 1995). Research has demonstrated a connection between TCA treatment and small yet significant increases in heart rate and cardiac conduction in adults and children (Wilens, Biederman, Baldessarini, Geller, Schleifer, Spencer et al., 1996), and there have been reports of sudden deaths associated with the cardiac effects from TCAs (e.g., Riddle, Nelson, Kleinman, Rasmusson, Leckman, King, & Cohen, 1991). Wilens et al. (2000b) recommend electrocardiographic measurements at baseline, during TCA treatment, and following cessation of TCAs to monitor the extent of impact on cardiac activity.

Ma, Lee, and Stafford (2005) note that antidepressants are often prescribed to children and adolescents even when if a specific drug has not been approved by the FDA. The only SSRI that has been approved for children under the age of 18 years is fluoxetine (Prozac). Furthermore, antidepressant medications produce an increased risk for suicidality in both children and adults (Healy & Aldred, 2005). This potential mandates that utmost caution be used in prescribing and carefully monitoring the effects of these agents when prescribed to children and adolescents.

Perhaps the most daunting obstacle to successful treatment is a lack of adherence on the part of the patient. Stine (1994) has examined the extant literature and has determined that fewer than 50% of adults or children treated for ADHD demonstrate compliance to treatment after six to nine months. In a study that assessed records of every prescription for methylphenidate for children in a New York county over a one-year period, Sherman and Hertzig (1991) reported that over one-half (52%) of the children who received methylphenidate prescriptions obtained only one prescription over the course of the year, thus making them adherent to treatment for a one month period of time. Health care professionals should evaluate issues related to compliance for every individual and family. Often, different individuals within families may not agree on a treatment plan, and dissenting opinions can prevent consistent approaches to the management of the disorder. When such dynamics are evaluated at the outset of treatment, compliance may be much improved.

**Lack of adherence to the treatment plan by the patient is common, and can compromise successful treatment**

Several issues influence the management of the adverse side effects associated with medication administration. Changing the dose or type of medication may ameliorate some of these adverse side effects. In order to mitigate the appetite disturbances often observed in individuals receiving stimulant medications, it is advised that individuals take their medications prior to breakfast and after dinner (Silver, 1992). Another potential barrier to adherence with the use of stimulants – or for that matter any medication – is economics. Sometimes, psychotropic interventions pose a financial burden that may be associated with the type of medication being prescribed, the number of daily doses to be administered, and how often refills need to be obtained. Frequently, individuals may not respond to one type of stimulant medication, yet may be assisted by another stimulant. Parents and teachers may overemphasize the benefits they observe as a result of stimulant medication, and discount the unpleasant experiences children may suffer. Thus, careful monitoring of the benefits of medication and their potential adverse effects are imperative.

The importance of accurately assessing ADHD is paramount when considering medication. For instance, Wilens et al. (2000b) note that learning disorders are not ameliorated by psychotropic medications. In another example, children who reside in violent or abusive environments will continue to experience the difficulties with attention and concentration that may represent adaptive coping strategies to the stressors associated with such environments. A comprehensive evaluation that provides a differential diagnoses is essential prior to recommending for psychotropic drug use.

## Summary

A range of treatments is available for individuals with ADHD. Individuals with ADHD and their families should receive information about the available options pertaining to the various available therapies in order to determine which treatment approach may best serve the needs of each individual patient given the presenting constellation of symptoms. There is considerable research that has demonstrated the efficacy of stimulant medication for ADHD, although these medications do not always improve functional outcomes (e.g., academic achievement; relationships) for children and adults with ADHD. Psychosocial treatments, particularly behavioral therapy, have received empirical support. In particular, cognitive behavioral techniques appear to increase adult patients' abilities to cope with ADHD symptoms and develop new mental and behavioral strategies. For young children, psychosocial interventions are most effective when they include parent training. School-aged children have been found to respond to behavioral approaches that are implemented both at home and in the classroom setting.

Combinations of psychosocial and psychopharmacologic interventions are often most effective, although empirical research has not always born this out (MTA Cooperative Group, 2004). A combined approach may promote parent and teacher acceptance of ADHD and contribute to greater adherence with treatment efforts. Most importantly, the integration of stimulant and psychosocial interventions seems to lower the medication dosage necessary to obtain the desired changes to a greater extent than stimulant therapy alone (Carlson et al., 1992). Although patients with ADHD report benefits from several psychological and technological interventions, much more research needs to be conducted to ascertain the elements of such approaches that are most helpful.

# 5

# Case Vignettes

## Case 1: Emilia

Emilia is a 10-year-old Hispanic girl who arrives with her aunt Anna for her first visit at the Mental Health Center. Anna is Emilia's legal guardian and is concerned that Emilia is failing school. A teacher has suggested that Emilia may have ADHD.

According to Emilia's aunt, who has raised her from birth, Emilia was born prematurely to a mother who abused drugs and alcohol during pregnancy. Emilia was a colicky infant who was difficult to feed, but has had no other major problems after birth and has been healthy except for a few early ear infections. She has since developed into a social child with boundless energy who is active in many sports at school.

Beginning in kindergarten, Emilia had difficulty is sustaining attention in school tasks or play activities, and every teacher she has had since that time has made this observation. At age six she could not read simple words but nonetheless her progress in reading was adequate through elementary school. Although the school has never provided Emilia with an evaluation or services, Anna has been helping significantly by structuring Emilia's approach to her schoolwork and by paying for private tutoring.

Emilia recently has been asking Anna why she cannot live with her mother. Anna responds that Emilia's mother is a high school dropout who is often in trouble with the law and has been unable to keep a job. Right now nobody knows where she lives. Lately, Emilia has been having difficulty falling asleep and is hard to arouse in the morning. Her appetite has been poor although she insists she is not hungry. When asked she denies suicidal thoughts. Her grades had been average until last year, when she started to fail a number of courses.

During her physical exam, Emilia was found to be in the 65th percentile for height, weight, and head circumference. Vital signs, vision screening, and hearing screening were normal and she has no dysmorphic features. The only dermatologic finding is pierced ears. Her neurologic exam was normal. Emilia was articulate and answered questions willingly.

At Emilia's next visit Anna brought, as requested, the completed Vanderbilt ratings scales, school records, schoolwork, and psychological evaluations. After reviewing these, it was determined that Emilia met the criteria for ADHD-1A, and she screened positive for anxiety and depression on Anna's version of the scale. On the teachers version however, Emilia did not meet the criteria for ADHD; however, she did meet the criteria for anxiety and depression.

After talking with Emilia's teachers, and considering her age, gender, and ethnicity, it is determined that Emilia has ADHD-1A. Because of the

Vanderbilt results, there is also concern about depression. In talking with Emilia, it is determined that she is not actively suicidal. Furthermore, it is known that some depressive symptoms in children with ADHD decrease in response to medication and improved performance in school. In consultation with Anna and Emilia, it is decided to begin medication for ADHD and to track Emilia's depression.

Because there is also concern about Emilia's reading problems, an assessment for an individualized educational program (IEP) through the school district is initiated. Additional evaluation from the school psychologist as part of the IEP process identifies a reading disorder for which Emilia has been compensating with her high intelligence and her aunt's help. The psychologist also notes increasing depression despite medication for ADHD, and improvement in Emilia's classroom performance, and wonders if treatment for depression is indicated. Because Emilia's scholastic performance has improved after starting medication, without a corresponding reduction in her depressive symptoms, it is decided that the depression should be treated. Emilia's aunt is upset because these problems were not identified earlier.

Emilia's history is typical of many cases of ADHD. She has some signs of depression, but is not severely impaired by her depressive symptoms; the decision to follow those symptoms while treating her ADHD is appropriate, as is the subsequent decision to treat her for depression when the depressive symptoms failed to improve. She also has a history that suggests a learning problem, i.e., a delay in reading simple words and specific challenges in this area, compared with other subjects. It is unclear whether Emilia has a learning disability that requires intervention through school-based services. In general, a history of developmental delay (including speech and language problems as a toddler, delayed phonetic awareness, and late acquisition of reading skills) requires comprehensive psychoeducational testing. Variable daily school performance in all subjects is more typical of ADHD, whereas poor academics or spotty performance across subjects may indicate a learning disability. A learning assessment that includes evaluation of reading, writing, mathematics, spelling, auditory and visual processing, and short- term memory should be performed by special education assessment personnel in the public school system, or by a clinician or clinical psychologist specializing in psycho-educational evaluation.

## Case 2: Andrea

Andrea is a Caucasian 19-year-old student in the second term of her first year at college. Although she reported expending a great deal of effort in her coursework, Andrea had received failing grades on her midterms in two science courses. She made an appointment at the counseling center on campus to discuss her academic difficulties. Andrea had always been interested in biology and had been considering a career in medicine, but after her struggles with her chemistry and biology classes, she wondered whether she needed to change her major and professional plans. Andrea described an active social life, and has felt the strain of competing academic and social pressures.

During elementary school, junior high, and high school, Andrea found that she could easily excel in her classes without having to allocate very much time for studying and assignments. She reports having been distracted often during classes and daydreaming during lectures, and often needed to check in with her classmates regarding course material or instructions that she missed. However, Andrea explained that she was able to perform well when the course content involved lab work with specific instructions and procedures, and that she has always remembered having had an intuitive sense regarding scientific mechanisms and processes. She thrives on "hands-on" activities, but often finds reading difficult. When she was assigned novels in her English classes, she always hoped that there would be a movie she could rent to help her visualize the book's content. After Andrea saw the movie, she found it much easier to read and remember passages in the novel. Besides these academic concerns, Andrea does not feel that other areas of her life have been especially challenging, except for her difficulties with organization. She has trouble keeping track of important papers, and often loses clothing or other items.

Andrea found the first term of college to be much more challenging than high school, and her academic performance has been a disappointment to her. However, during her initial term, she attended the college's freshman seminar program, and received quite a bit of individual attention, which she says was quite helpful. During the current term, she is enrolled in two large lecture classes and two smaller seminar classes. Although some of the material from lectures is accessible in the textbooks, Andrea feels she cannot maintain her attention during the lectures and take adequate notes. She feels competent during the lab sections, and has received high grades for her lab reports, but has failed the multiple-choice tests that comprise a major portion of her grade in both courses. Andrea is especially upset about this, because she feels that in some cases, she understood the material that appeared on the tests, but could not recall it at the time.

Andrea also describes some strain in balancing her social life with her academic objectives, and notes that her academic failures have influenced her sense of identity. In high school, she had a group of friends that tended to socialize together. In college, Andrea has made several new friends in her dormitory and in her classes, but finds that she often forgets social events that she had planned. Although at times she has forgotten or cancelled social plans because of her schoolwork, she describes being so upset about her academic difficulties, that she has increased her socializing and feels that spending time with friends offers a positive escape from her academic concerns. She also explained that she feels "like a failure" and that her sense of herself as a capable student has been seriously disrupted.

One of Andrea's friends has ADHD, and takes a stimulant medication. This friend offered her a dose of the medication, which she tried before a chemistry lecture. She noticed that her concentration and grasp of that lecture's material seemed to come more easily than usual. Andrea wondered whether ADHD might be responsible for some of her difficulties. Her goal in coming to the counseling center was to obtain an evaluation for ADHD and to determine whether medication might be helpful.

At the college counseling center, Andrea participated in a full assessment for ADHD, which included the Brown ADHD scales and interview, the WAIS-

III, and the TOVA. Andrea's mother was able to provide information in an interview over the phone about her childhood behaviors. She also completed a checklist of Andrea's symptoms, and faxed some of her old school report cards to the counseling center. Andrea's mother and several of her high school teachers identified her difficulties with organization and a tendency to be easily distracted. Andrea also noted these difficulties herself during the interview from the Brown scales. Her TOVA and WAIS-III scores were consistent with those of individuals with ADHD. Following this assessment, Andrea was referred to a psychiatrist who prescribed Adderall to target her attentional difficulties. She also had three counseling sessions at the student health center, which targeted her disappointment in her coursework and its effects on her identity. The counseling sessions also gave her the confidence to take the initiative to form study groups for her biology and chemistry classes, which contribute to her improved performance in those courses.

Andrea's case is typical of many new college students who managed to succeed in high school, but who struggle to adjust to more demanding academic and social expectations during college. Levels of secondary education vary, and many students come to college from high schools with minimal academic standards. In these cases, some individuals with ADHD may have been able to function well during high school with minor adaptations, but find that college presents challenges that extend beyond to the studying habits and coping mechanisms to which they were accustomed. This type of student is unlikely to have received a diagnosis of ADHD before reaching college, but may be helped by psychosocial and pharmacological interventions.

## Case 3: Peter

Peter is a 34-year-old African-American male who works in software development. He describes himself as having ADHD and he believes that his grades in school were seriously compromised by his difficulties with attention and concentration. He also described being "fidgety" and having had trouble sitting still for long periods of time. Until Peter was diagnosed with ADHD in the ninth grade, his parents repeatedly chastised him for what they perceived as his lack of motivation and effort. Peter began taking stimulant medication in the ninth grade, and found that it helped his ADHD symptoms of inattention, but he still had trouble controlling his impulsivity. He continued taking the medication in college, but stopped after college, when his work environments did not necessitate the same sorts of prolonged attention that had been necessary for his academic coursework.

Peter has worked at the same company for six years. When he began to work for his current employer, it was a startup company. Peter's job involved multiple tasks, including establishing the structure and framework for software systems, testing his company's products, developing new versions of the software, backing up the software periodically, writing scripts to automate deployment, and creating the user interface. With only four coworkers, Peter's role was rather fluid, and he "wore multiple hats." He enjoyed the variety in his work and the continual interaction with his colleagues. Peter was able to switch tasks according to his ideas and interests. The company became quite successful, and Peter felt capable and proud of his work.

As the company grew, Peter's job description became more specific. He was made the manager of a particular sub-area. His new job demanded that he focus exclusively on "release control" – making sure that there were no "bugs" in the current version of the company's software.

Peter has begun to get quite bored at work, and finds that his concentration is wandering. He finds himself taking many breaks throughout the day. In addition, Peter cannot help working on projects to which he is not assigned. Though many of his coworkers appreciate his unsolicited feedback, others do not, and the work in his own department has not been up to his usual performance. Though on one level, Peter is aware that his ADHD may be related to his current difficulties, he has noticed that he has begun to view himself as lazy and unsuccessful, and to re-experience some of the negative messages about his character that he experienced while growing up. He has begun to feel rather depressed, and notes that he is not as interested in spending time with his girlfriend, his friends, and his family as he used to be.

Peter made an appointment for therapy to address his depressive feelings and to discuss whether he should resume taking ADHD medication. His assessment included neuropsychological measures, including the WAIS-III and the CPT. It also included an extensive interview regarding Peter's employment history that included his relationships with colleagues and bosses, his work satisfaction among different tasks and jobs, and his interests and goals. The results indicated that Peter had many of the typical neuropsychological correlates of ADHD. From his responses, it became clear that Peter excels in situations where his responsibilities span several domains and require that he integrate these topic areas. He also enjoys work that promises continued challenges and a degree of novelty.

Peter's therapy explored the interactions among his work situation, his cognitive strengths and weaknesses, and his personal life. Eventually, he was able to rework his position within the company to be more similar to his initial one, and again experienced interest and satisfaction at work and an alleviation of his depressive symptoms.

# 6

# Further Reading

Barkley, R. A. (1997). *ADHD and the nature of self-control*. New York: Guilford. This book provides a comprehensive overview of the research on the etiology and presentation of ADHD. In particular, it considers the influences of executive function and behavioral inhibition on psychological functioning and behavior. Though it primarily addresses the cognitive factors related to the disorder, the book includes a chapter on the social and clinical issues relevant to ADHD.

Barkley, R. A. (2005). *Taking charge of ADHD: The complete, authoritative guide for parents*. New York: Guilford. This book synthesizes the most current research about ADHD and the most effective treatment approaches. It is particularly helpful in explaining the necessity for treatment informed by scientific research, and in encouraging parents to examine their previous beliefs and judgments about the disorder. The information is clearly presented and includes concrete suggestions and tools. Though intended for parents, it may also be helpful for patients and clinicians.

Brown, T. E. (Ed.). (2000). *Attention deficit disorders and comorbidities in children, adolescents, and adults*. Washington, DC: American Psychiatric Press, Inc. This edited volume brings together contributions from the leading ADHD researchers who present authoritative chapters on the etiology, diagnosis, and treatment of ADHD and its presentation and course with comorbid disorders. Chapters address the comorbidity of ADHD with affective disorders, anxiety, learning disorders, conduct and oppositional/defiant disorders, and examine other topics such as pharmacology and ADHD across different age groups.

Rieff, M. I., & Tippins, S. (2004). *ADHD: A complete and authoritative guide*. Oak Grove Village, IL: American Association of Pediatrics. Primarily for parents of children with ADHD, this book offers a concise summary of the issues facing parents, patients and clinicians today as they form an understanding of ADHD and make treatment choices. It also discusses the history of the disorder and evaluates alternative approaches to treatment.

Weiss, M., Hechtman, L. T., & Weiss, G. (1999). *ADHD in adulthood: A guide to current theory, diagnosis, and treatment*. Baltimore, MD: The Johns Hopkins University Press. This work is the major source for approaches to ADHD with adults. It will help providers understand how the disorder affects adults, including its effects on careers and relationships. The book provides thorough discussions of treatment issues, including detailed considerations of psychotherapeutic processes and suggestions for medication management.

# 7

# References

Abikoff, H., Hechtman, L., Klein, R. G., Gallagher, R., Fleiss, K., Etcovitch, J., et al. (2004). Social functioning in children with ADHD treated with long-term methylphenidate and multimodal psychosocial treatment. *Journal of the American Academy of Child and Adolescent Psychiatry, 43*(7), 820–829.

Achenbach, T. M., Howell, C. T., McConaughy, S. H., & Stanger, C. (1995). Six-year predictors of problems in a national sample, III: Transitions to adult syndromes. *Journal of the American Academy of Child and Adolescent Psychiatry, 34*, 658–669.

Adler, L. A. (2004). Clinical presentations with adult patients with ADHD. *Journal of Clinical Psychiatry, 64*(Suppl. 3), 8–11.

American Academy of Pediatrics. (2000). Clinical practice guideline: Diagnosis and evaluation of a child with attention-deficit/hyperactivity disorder. *Pediatrics, 105*, 1158–1170.

American Psychiatric Association. (2000). *Diagnostic and statistical manual of mental disorders* (4th ed., text revision). Washington, DC: Author.

Anastopoulos, A., Shelton, T., & Barkley, R. A. (2005). Family-based psychosocial treatments for children and adolescents with attention-deficit/hyperactivity disorder. In E. D. Hibbs & P. S. Jensen (Eds.), *Psychosocial treatments for child and adolescent disorders: Empirically based strategies for clinical practice* (pp. 327–350). Washington, DC: American Psychological Association.

Anastopoulos, A. D., Shelton, T. L., DuPaul, G. J., & Guevremont, D. C. (1993). Parent training for attention-deficit/hyperactivity disorder: Its impact on parent functioning. *Journal of Abnormal Child Psychology, 21*, 581–596.

Antshel, K. M., & Remer, R. (2003). Social skills training in children with attention deficit hyperactivity disorder: A randomized-controlled clinical trial. *Journal of Clinical Child and Adolescent Psychology, 32*(1), 152–165.

Arnold, L. E. (1997). Sex differences in ADHD: Conference summary. *Journal of Abnormal Child Psychology, 24*, 555–569.

Arnold, L. E. (2001). Alternative treatments for adults with attention-deficit hyperactivity disorder (ADHD). *The Annals of the New York Academy of Sciences, 931*, 310–341.

Arnsten, A. (1999). Development of the cerebral cortex: XIV: Stress impairs prefrontal cortical function. *Journal of the American Academy of Child and Adolescent Psychiatry, 38*(2), 220–222.

Babcock, H. (1930). An experiment in the measurement of mental deterioration. *Archives of Psychology, 117*, 105.

Barkley, R. A. (1989). The problem of stimulus control and rule-governed behavior in children with attention deficit disorder with hyperactivity. In J. Swanson & L. Bloomingdale (Eds.), *Attention deficit disorders* (pp. 203–234). New York: Pergamon Press.

Barkley, R. A. (1990). *Attention deficit hyperactivity disorder: A handbook for diagnosis and treatment*. New York: Guilford.

Barkley, R. A. (1998a). *Attention deficit hyperactivity disorder: A clinical workbook* (2nd ed.). New York: Guilford Press.

Barkley, R. A. (1998b). *Attention deficit hyperactivity disorder: A handbook for diagnosis and treatment*. New York: Guilford Press.

Barkley, R. A. (2006). *Attention-deficit hyperactivity: A handbook for diagnosis and treatment* (3rd ed.). New York: Guilford Press.

Barkley, R. A., Grodzinsky, G., & DuPaul, G. J. (1992). Frontal lobe function in attention deficit disorder with and without hyperactivity: a review and research report. *Journal of Abnormal Child Psychology, 20*(2), 163–188.

Barkley, R. A., Murphy, K. R., & Kwasnik, D. (1996). Psychological adjustment and adaptive impairments in young adults with ADHD. *Journal of Attention Disorders, 1*, 41–54.

Barkley, R. A., Murphy K. R., O'Connell T., & Connor D. F. (2005). Effects of two doses of methylphenidate on simulator driving performance in adults with attention deficit hyperactivity disorder. *Journal of Safety Research, 36*, 121–131.

Beck, A. T. (1990). *Beck Anxiety Inventory*. San Antonio, TX: Psychological Corporation.

Beck, A. T., Steer, R. A., & Brown, G. K. (1996). *Beck Depression Inventory-II*. San Antonio, TX: The Psychological Corporation.

Becker-Blease, K. A., Freyd, J. J., & Pears, K. C. (2004). Preschoolers' memory for threatening information depends on trauma history and attentional context: Implications for the development of dissociation. *Journal of Trauma and Dissociation, 5*(1), 113–131.

Behar, D., Rapoport, J. L., Adams, A. J., Berg, C. J, & Cornblath, M. (1989). Sugar challenge testing with children behavior: Results from the Edinburgh lead study. *Journal of Child Psychology and Psychiatry, 30*, 515–528.

Bennett, F. C., Brown, R. T., Craver, J., & Anderson, D. (1999). Stimulant medication for the child with attention-deficit/hyperactivity disorder. *Pediatric Clinics of North America, 46*(5), 929–944.

Berg, E. A. (1948). A simple objective treatment for measuring flexibility in thinking. *Journal of General Psychology, 39*, 15–22.

Biederman, J., Baldessarini, R. J., Wright, V., Knee, D., & Harmatz, J. (1989). A double-blind placebo controlled study of desipramine in the treatment of attention deficit disorder, I: Efficacy. *Journal of the American Academy of Child and Adolescent Psychiatry, 28*, 777–784.

Biederman, J., Baldessarini, R. J., Wright, V., Keenan K., & Faraone, S. (1993). A double-blind placebo controlled study of desipramine in the treatment of attention deficit disorder, III: Lack of impact of comorbidity and family history factors on clinical response. *Journal of the American Academy of Child and Adolescent Psychiatry, 32*, 199–204.

Biederman, J., Faraone, S. V., & Lapey, K. (1992). Comorbidity of diagnosis in attention-deficit hyperactivity disorder. *Child and Adolescent Clinics of North America, 1*(2), 335–360.

Biederman, J., Faraone, S. V., Spencer, T., Wilens, T., Norman, D., Lapey, K. A., et al. (1993). Patterns of psychiatric comorbidity, cognition, and psychosocial functioning in adults with attention deficit disorder. *American Journal of Psychiatry, 150*, 1972–1978.

Biederman, J., Lopez, F. A., Boellner, S. W., & Chandler, M. C. (2002). A randomized, double-blind, placebo-controlled, parallel-group study of SL1391 (Adderall XR) in children with attention-deficit /hyperactivity disorder. *Pediatrics, 110*, 258–286.

Biederman, J., Swanson, J. M., Wigal., S. B., Kratochvil, C. J., Boellner, S. W., Earl, C.Q., et al. (2005). Efficacy and safety of modafinil film-coated tablets in children and adolescents with attention-deficit/hyperactivity disorder: results of a randomized, double-blind, placebo-controlled, flexible-dose study [Electronic version]. *Pediatrics, 116*(6), 777–784.

Biederman, J., Thisted, R. A., Greenhill, L. L., & Ryan, N. D. (1995). Estimation of the association between desipramine and the risk for sudden death in 5- to 14-year-old children. *Journal of Clinical Psychiatry, 56*(3), 87–93.

Biederman, J., Wilens, T. E., Mick, E., Spencer, T., & Faraone, S. V. (1999). Protective effects of ADHD pharmacotherapy on subsequent substance abuse: A longitudinal study [Electronic version]. *Pediatrics, 104*(2), 20.

Bor, W., Sanders, M. R., & Markie-Dadds, C. (2002). The effects of the Triple-P Positive Parenting Program on preschool children with co-occurring disruptive behavior and attentional/hyperactivity difficulties. *Journal of Abnormal Child Psychology, 30*(6), 571–587.

Breslau, N., Brown, G. G., DelDotto, J. E., Kumar, S., Ezhuthachan, S., Andreski, P., & Hufnagle, K. G. (1996). Psychiatric sequelae of low birth weight at 6 years of age. *Journal of Abnormal Child Psychology, 3*, 385–400.

Brestan, E. V., & Eyberg, S. M. (1998). Effective psychosocial treatments of conduct disordered children and adolescents: 29 years, 82 studies, and 5772 kids. *Journal of Clinical Child Psychology, 27*, 180–189.

Brown, R. T., Antonuccio, D., DuPaul, G., Fristad, M., King, C., Leslie, L., et al. (in press). *Report of the working group on psychotropic medications for children adolescents: Psychopharmacological, psychosocial, and combined interventions for childhood disorders: Evidence base, contextual factors and future directions.* Washington, DC: American Psychological Association.

Brown, R. T., & Daly, B. (in press). Neuropsychological effects of stimulant medication on children's learning and behavior. In C.R. Reynolds & E. Fletcher-Janzen (Eds., 3rd ed.), *Handbook of clinical neuropsychology.* New York: Plenum Press.

Brown, R. T., Dreelin, E., & Dingle, A. D. (1997). Neuropsychological effects of stimulant medication on children's learning and behavior. In C. R. Reynolds & E. Fletcher-Janzen (Eds.), *Handbook of clinical child neuropsychology* (pp. 539–572). New York: Plenum Press.

Brown, R. T., & La Rosa, A. (2002). Recent developments in the pharmamacotherapy of attention-deficit/hyperactivity disorder (ADHD). *Professional Psychology: Research and Practice, 33*(6), 591–595.

Brown, R. T., & Sammons, M. T. (2003). Pediatric psychopharmacology: A review of new developments and recent research. *Professional Psychology: Research and Practice, 33*, 135–147.

Brown, R. T., & Sawyer, M. G. (1998). *Medications for school-age children: Effects on learning and behavior.* New York: Guilford.

Brown, T. E. (1996). *Brown Attention-Deficit Disorder Scales: Manual.* Toronto: The Psychological Corporation.

Brown, T. E. (2000). Emerging understandings of attention-deficit disorders and co-morbidities. In T. E. Brown (Ed.), *Attention-deficit disorders and comorbidities in children, adolescents, and adults* (pp. 3–55). Washington, DC: American Psychiatric Press, Inc.

Bukstein, O. G., & Kolko, D. J. (1998). Effects of methylphenidate on aggressive urban children with attention deficit hyperactivity disorder. *Journal of Clinical and Child Psychology, 27*, 340–351.

Burt, S. A., Krueger, R. F., McGue, M., & Iacono, W. (2003). Parent-child conflict and the comorbidity among childhood externalizing disorders. *Archives of General Psychiatry, 60*(5), 505–513.

Campbell, S. B. (1990). *Behavior problems in preschool children.* New York: Guilford Press.

Carlson, C. L., Pelham, W. E., Milich, R., & Dixon, M. J. (1992). Single and combined effects of methylphenidate and behavior therapy on the classroom behavior, academic performance and self-evaluations of children with attention deficit-hyperactivity disorder. *Journal of Abnormal Child Psychology, 20*, 213–232.

Castellanos, F. X., Giedd, J. N., Eckburg, P., Marsh, W. L., Vaituzis, C., Kaysen, D., et al. (1994). Quantitative morphology of the caudate nucleus in attention deficit hyperactivity disorder. *American Journal of Psychiatry, 151*, 1791–1796.

Castellanos, F. X., Giedd, J. N., Marsh, W. L., Hamburger, S. D., Vaitzuzis, A. C., Dickstein, D. P., et al. (1996). Quantitative brain magnetic resonance imaging in attention-deficit hyperactivity disorder. *Archives of General Psychiatry, 53*, 607–616.

Charach, A., Ickowicz, A., & Schachar, R. (2004). Stimulant treatment over five years: Adherence, effectiveness, and adverse effects. *Journal of the American Academy of Child and Adolescent Psychiatry, 43*, 559–567.

Cohen, M. (1997). *Children's Memory Scale.* San Antonio, TX: Psychological Corporation.

Comings, D. E. (2000). Attention-deficit/hyperactivity disorder with Tourette syndrome. In T. E. Brown (Ed.), *Attention deficit disorders and comorbidities in children, adolescents, and adults* (pp. 363–391). Washington, DC: American Psychiatric Press, Inc.

Conners, C. K. (1980). *Food additives and hyperactive children.* New York: Plenum Press.

Conners, C. K. (1985). The computerized continuous performance test. *Psychopharmacology Bulletin, 21,* 891–892.

Conners, C. K. (2001). *Conners rating scales revised: Technical manual.* North Tonawanda, NY: Multi-Health Systems, Inc.

Constantino, J. N., Liberman, M., & Kincaid, M. (1997). Effects of serotonin reuptake inhibitors on aggressive behavior in psychiatrically hospitalized adolescents: Results of an open trial. *Journal of Child and Adolescent Psychopharmacology, 7,* 31–44.

Cook, E. H. (2000). Molecular genetic studies of attention-deficit/hyperactivity disorder. In P. J. Accardo, T. A. Blondis, B. Y. Whitman, & M. A. Stein (Eds.), *Attention deficits and hyperactivity in children and adults* (pp. 13–27). New York: Marcel Dekker, Inc.

Counts, C. A., Nigg, J. T., Stawicki, J. A., Rappley, M. D., & von Eye, A. (2005). Family adversity in DSM-IV ADHD combined and inattentive subtypes and associated disruptive behavior problems. *American Academy of Child and Adolescent Psychiatry, 44*(7), 690–698.

Delis, D. C., Kramer, J., Kaplan. E., & Ober, B. (1987). *The California Verbal Learning Test.* New York: Psychologyical Corporation.

Denckla, M. B. (2000). Learning disabilities and attention-deficit/hyperactivity disorder in adults: Overlap with executive dysfunction. In T. E. Brown (Ed.), *Attention-deficit disorders and comorbidities in children, adolescents, and adults* (pp. 297–318). Washington, DC: American Psychiatric Press, Inc.

Derogatis, L. R. (1975). *Symptom Checklist-90-Revised.* Minneapolis, MN: NCS Assessments.

Diamond, I. R., Tannock, R., & Schachar, R. J. (1999). Response to methylphenidate in children with ADHD and comorbid anxiety. *Journal of the Academy of Child and Adolescent Psychiatry, 38,* 402–409.

Douglas, V. I. (1983). Attention and cognitive problems. In M. Rutter (Ed.), *Developmental neuropsychiatry* (pp. 280–329). New York: Guilford Press.

DuPaul, G. J. (1991). Parent and teacher ratings of ADHD symptoms: Psychometric properties in a community-based sample. *Journal of Clinical Child Psychology, 20,* 245–253.

DuPaul, G. J., Barkley, R., & McMurray, M. (1994). Response of children with ADHD to methylphenidate: Interaction with internalizing symptoms. *Journal of the American Academy of Child and Adolescent Psychiatry, 33,* 894–903.

DuPaul, G. J., & Eckert, T. L. (1997). The effects of school-based interventions for attention-deficit/hyperactivity disorder: A meta-analysis. *School Psychology Review, 26,* 5–27.

DuPaul, G. J., & Rapport, M. D. (1993). Does methylphenidate normalize the classroom performance of children with attention deficit disorder? *Journal of the American Academy of Child and Adolescent Psychiatry, 32,* 190–198.

DuPaul, G. J., & Stoner, G. (2003). *ADHD in the schools: Assessment and intervention strategies.* New York: Guilford.

Efron, D., Jarman, F. C., & Barker, M. J. (1997). Methylphenidate versus dexamphetamine in children with attention deficit hyperactivity disorder: A double-blind crossover trial [Electronic version]. *Pediatrics, 100,* 6.

Elia, J. Welsh, P. A. Gullotta, C. S., & Rapoport, J. L. (1993). Classroom academic performance: Improvement with both methylphenidate and dextroamphetamine in ADHD boys. *Journal of Child Psychology and Psychiatry, 34,* 785–804.

Elliott, H. (2002). Attention deficit hyperactivity disorder in adults: A guide for the primary care physician. *Southern Medical Journal, 95,* 736–742.

Erdman, P. (1998). Conceptualizing ADHD as a contextual response to parental attachment. *American Journal of Family Therapy, 26*(2), 177–185.

Faraone, S. V. (2004). Genetics of adult attention-deficit/hyperactivity disorder. *Psychiatric Clinics of North America, 27*(2), 303–321.

Faraone, S. V., Biederman, J., Mennin, D., Wozniak, J., & Spencer, T. (1997). Attention deficit hyperactivity disorder with bipolar disorder: A familial subtype? *American Academy of Child and Adolescent Psychiatry, 36,* 1378–1387.

Feingold, B. (1985). *Why your child is hyperactive*. New York: Random House.

Findling, R. L. (1996). Open-label treatment of comorbid depression and attentional disorders with co-administration of serotonin reuptake inhibitors and psychostimulants in children, adolescents, and adults: A case series. *Journal of Child and Adolescent Psychopharmocology, 6*, 165–175.

Ford, J. D., Racusin, R., Ellis, C. G., Daviss, W. B., Reiser, J., Fleischer, A., & Thomas, J. (2000). Child maltreatment, other trauma exposure and posttraumatic symptomatology among children with oppositional defiant and attention deficit hyperactivity disorders. *Child Maltreatment: Journal of the American Professional Society on the Abuse of Children, 5*(3), 205–217.

Gadow, K. D., Nolan, E. E., & Sverd, J. (1992). Methylphenidate in hyperactive boys with comorbid tic disorder, II: Short-term behavioral effects in school setting. *Journal of the American Academy of Child and Adolescent Psychiatry, 31*, 462–471.

Gammon, G. D., & Brown, T. E. (1993). Fluoxetine and methylphenidate in combination for treatment of attention deficit disorder and comorbid depressive disorder. *Journal of Child and Adolescent Psychopharmacology, 3*, 1–10.

Geurts, H. M., Verte, S., Oosterlaan, J., Roeyers, H., & Sergeant, J. A. (2005). ADHD subtypes: Do they differ in their executive functioning profile? *Archives of Clinical Neuropsychology, 20*(4), 457–77.

Giedd, J. N., Blumenthal., J., Molloy, E., & Castellanos, F. X. (2001). Brain imaging of attention-deficit/hyperactivity disorder. *Annals of the New York Academy of Science, 931*, 33–49.

Gittelman, R., & Abikoff, H. (1989). The role of psychostimulants and psychosocial treatments in hyperkinesis. In T. Sagvolden & T. Archer (Eds.), *Attention deficit disorder: Clinical and basic research* (pp. 167–180). Hillsdale, NJ: Erlbaum.

Gol, D., & Jarus, T. (2005). Effect of a social skills training group on everyday activities of children with attention-deficit-hyperactivity disorder. *Developmental Medicine and Child Neurology, 7*(8), 539–545.

Golden, C. J. (1978). *Stroop color and word test manual*. Chicago: Stoelting.

Gordon, M. (1986). How is a computerized attention test used in the diagnosis of attention deficit disorder? *Journal of Children in Contemporary Society, 19*(1–2), 53–64.

Grcevich, S., Rowane, W. A., & Marcellino, B. (2001). Retrospective comparison of Adderall and Methylphenidate in the treatment of attention deficit hyperactivity disorder. *Journal of Child & Adolescent Psychopharmacology, 11*, 35–41.

Greenberg, L. M., & Waldman, I. D. (1993). Developmental normative data on the Test of Variables of Attention. *Journal of Child Psychology and Psychiatry, 4*, 1019–1030.

Gronwall, D. (1977). Paced auditory serial addition task: A measure of recovery from concussion. *Percept Motor Skills, 44*, 367–373.

Hall, K. M., Irwin, M. M., Bowman, K. A., Frankenberger, W., & Jewett, D. C. (2005). Illicit use of prescribed stimulant medication among college students. *Journal of American College Health, 53*(4), 167–74.

Hammill, D. D., Brown, V. L., Larsen, S. C., & Wiederhold, J. L. (1994). *Test of Adolescent and Adult Language* (3rd ed.). Austin, TX: Pro-Ed.

Hartman, R. R., Stage, S. A., & Webster-Stratton, C. (2003). A growth curve analysis of parent training outcomes: Examining the influence of child risk factors (inattention, impulsivity, and hyperactivity problems), parental and family risk factors. *Journal of Child Psychology and Psychiatry and Allied Disciplines, 44*, 388–398.

Havey, J. M., Olson, J. M., McCormick, C., & Cates, G. L. (2005). Teachers' perceptions of the incidence and management of attention-deficit hyperactivity disorder. *Applied Neuropsychology, 12*(2), 120-127.

Healy, D., & Aldred, G. (2005). Antidepressant drug use and the risk of suicide. *International Review of Psychiatry, 17*(3), 163–172.

Hechtman, L., Abikoff, H., Klein, R. G., Weiss, G., Respitz, C., Kouri, J., et al. (2004). Academic achievement and emotional status of children with ADHD treated with long-term methylphenidate and multimodal psychosocial treatment. *Journal of American Academy of Child and Adolescent Psychiatry, 43*(7), 812–819.

Hesslinger, B., Tebartz van Elst, L., Nyberg, E., Dykierek, P., Richter, H., Berner, & M., Ebert, D. (2002). Psychotherapy of attention deficit hyperactivity disorder in adults-a pilot study using a structured skills training program. *European Archives of Psychiatry and Clinical Neuroscience, 252*(4), 177–84.

Hinshaw, S. P. (1991). Stimulant medication and the treatment of aggression in children with attentional deficits. *Journal of Clinical Child Psychology, 20*, 301–312.

Hinshaw, S. P., Heller, T., & McHale, J. P. (1992). Covert antisocial behavior in boys with attention-deficit hyperactivity disorder: External validation and effects of methylphenidate. *Journal of Consulting and Clinical Psychology, 60*, 274–281.

Hinshaw, S. P., Henker, B., & Whalen, C. K. (1984). Self-control in hyperactive boys in anger-inducing situations: Effects of cognitive-behavioral training and of methylphenidate. *Journal of Abnormal Child Psychology, 12*, 155–177.

Hinshaw, S. P., Owens, E. B., Wells, K. C., & Abikoff, H. B. (2000). Family processes and treatment outcome in the MTA: Negative/ineffective parenting practices in relation to multimodal treatment. *Journal of Abnormal Child Psychology 6*, 555–568.

Hudziak, J. J., Rudiger, L. P. , Neale, M. C., Heath, A. C., & Todd, R. D. (2000). A twin study of inattentive, aggressive, and anxious/depressed behavior. *Journal of the American Academy of Child and Adolescent Psychiatry, 39*(4), 469–476.

Hynd, G. W., Hern, K. L., Novey, E. S ., Eliopulos. D., Marshall, R., Gonzalez, J. J., & Voeller, K. K. (1993). Attention-deficit hyperactivity disorder and asymmetry of the caudate nucleus. *Journal of Child Neurology, 8*, 339–347.

Hynd, G. W., Semrud-Clikeman, M., Lorys, A. R., Novey, E. S., Eliopulos. D., & Lyytinen, H. (1991). Corpus callosum morphology in attention-deficit-hyperactivity disorder: Morphometric analysis of MRI. *Journal of Learning Disabilities, 24*, 141–146.

Hynd, G. W., Semrud-Clikeman, M., Lorys, A. R., Novey, E. S., & Eliopulos. D. (1990). Brain morphology in developmental dyslexia in attention deficit hyperactivity disorder/hyperactivity. *Archives of Neurology, 47*, 919–926.

Ickowicz, A., Tannock, R., Fulford. P., Purvis, K., & Schachar, R. (1992). *Transient tics and compulsive behaviors following methylphenidate: Evidence from a placebo controlled double blind clinical trial.* American Academy of Child and Adolescent Psychiatry, 39th Annual Meeting, Washington, D.C.

Jadad, A. R., Booker, L., Gauld, M., Kakuma, R., Boyle, M., Cunningham, C. E. et al. (1999). The treatment of attention-deficit hyperactivity disorder: An annotated bibliography and critical appraisal of published systematic reviews and meta-analyses. *Canadian Journal of Psychiatry, 44*, 1025–1035.

Jensen, P. S., Hinshaw, S. P., Kraemer, H. C., Lenora, N., Newcorn, J. H., Abikoff, H. B.,et al. (2001). ADHD comorbidity findings from the MTA study: Comparing comorbid subgroups. *Journal of the American Academy of Child and Adolescent Psychiatry, 40*(2), 147–158.

Jester, J. M, Nigg, J. T., Adams, K., Fitzgerald, H. E., Puttler, L. I., Wong, M. M., & Zucker, R. A. (2005). Inattention/hyperactivity and aggression from early childhood to adolescence: Heterogeneity of trajectories and differential influence of family environment characteristics. *Development and Psychopathology, 17*, 99–125.

Kaplan, B. J., Crawford, S. G., Fisher, G. C., & Dewey, D. M. (1998). Family dysfunction is more strongly associated with ADHD than with general school problems. *Journal of Attention Disorders, 2*(4), 209–216.

Kaplan, S. L., Busner, J., Kupietz, S., Wassermann, E., & Segal, B. (1990). Effects of methylphenidate on adolescents with aggressive conduct disorder and ADHD: A preliminary report. *Journal of the American Academy of Child and Adolescent Psychiatry, 29*, 719–723.

Kempton, S., Vance, A., Maruff, P., Luk, E., Costin, J., & Pantelis, C. (1999). Executive function and attention deficit hyperactivity disorder: Stimulant medication and better executive function performance in children. *Psychological Medicine, 29*, 527–538.

Klein, R. G., Abikoff, H., Klass, E., Ganeles, D., Seese, L. M., & Pollack, S. (1997). Chemical efficacy of methylpenidate in conduct disorder with and without attention-deficit/hyperactivity disorder. *Archives of General Psychiatry, 54*, 1073–1086.

Klingberg, T., Fernell, E., Olesen, P. J., Johnson, M., Gustafsson, P., Dahlstrom, K., et al. (2005). Computerized training of working memory in children with ADHD: A randomized, controlled trial. *Journal of the American Academy of Child and Adolescent Psychiatry, 44*(2), 177–186.

Klorman, R., Brumaghim, J. T., Salzman, L. F., Strauss, J., Borgstedt, A. D., McBride, M. C., & Loeb, S. (1988). Effects of methylphenidate on attention-deficit/hyperactivity disorder with and without aggressive/noncompliant features. *Journal of Abnormal Psychology, 97*, 413–422.

Knopik, V. S., Sparrow, E. P., Madden, P. A., Bucholz, K. K., Hudziak, J. J., Reich, W., et al. (2005). Contributions of parental alcoholism, prenatal substance exposure, and genetic transmission to child ADHD risk: A female twin study. *Psychological Medicine, 25*(5), 625–35.

Kreppner, J. M., O'Connor, T. G., Rutter, M., Beckett, C., Castle, J., Croft, C., et al. (2001). Can inattention/overactivity be an institutional deprivation syndrome? *Journal of Abnormal Child Psychology, 29*(6), 513–528.

Lahey, B. B., McBurnett, K., & Loeber, R. (2000). Are attention-deficit/hyperactivity disorder and oppositional defiant disorder developmental precursors to conduct disorder? In A. J. Sameroff, M. Lewis, & S. M. Miller (Eds.), *Handbook of developmental psychopathology* (2nd ed., pp. 431–446). New York: Kluwer Academic/Plenum.

Levin, F. R., Evans, S. M., & Kleber, H. D. (1999). Alcohol and drug abuse: Practical guidelines for the treatment of substance abusers with adult attention-deficit/hyperactivity disorder. *Psychiatric Services, 50*(8), 1001–1003.

Lezak, M. (1995). Neuropsychological Assessment (3rd ed.). New York: Oxford University Press.

Loo, S. K., & Barkley, R. A. (2005). Clinical utility of EEG in attention deficit hyperactivity disorder. *Applied Neuropsychology, 12*(2), 64–76.

Losier, B. J., McGrath, P. J., & Klein, R. M. (1996). Error patterns on the Continuous Performance Test in non-medication and medicated samples of children with and without ADHD: A meta-analysis. *Journal of Child Psychology and Psychiatry, 37*, 971–987.

Lundahl, B., Risser, H. J., & Lovejoy, C. M. (2006). A meta-analysis of parent-training: Moderators and follow-up effects. *Clinical Psychology Review, 26*, 86–104.

Ma, J., Lee, K. V., & Stafford, R. S. (2005). Depression treatment during outpatient visits by U.S. children and adolescents. *Journal of Adolescent Health, 37*(6), 434–42.

Mannuzza, S., Klein, R., Bessler, A., Malloy, P., LaPadula, M., & Addalli, K. (1993). Adult outcome of hyperactive boys: Educational achievement, occupational rank, and psychiatric status. *Archives of General Psychiatry, 50*, 379–380.

Matier, K., Halperin, J. M., Sharma, V., Newcorn, J. H., & Sathaye, N. (1992). Methylphenidate response in aggressive and nonaggressive ADHD children: Distinctions on laboratory measures of symptoms. *Journal of the American Academy of Child and Adolescent Psychiatry, 31*, 219–225.

McElroy, S. L., Keck, P. E. Jr., Pope, H. G. Jr., Hudson, J. I., Faedda, G. L., & Swann, A. C. (1992). Clinical and research implications of the diagnosis of dysphoric or mixed mania or hypersomnia. *American Journal of Psychiatry, 145*, 221–223.

McMaster University Evidence-Based Practice Center. (1999). *Treatment of attention-deficit hyperactivity disorder*. Evidence Report/Technology Assessment no. 11, AHCPR Publication No. 99-E018. Rockville, MD: Agency for Health Care Policy & Research.

Mick, E., Biederman, J., Prince, J., Fischer, M. J., & Faraone, S. V. (2002). Impact of low birth weight on attention-deficit hyperactivity disorder. *Journal of Developmental and Behavioral Pediatrics, 23*(1), 16–22.

Mrug, S., Hoza, B., & Gerdes, A. C. Children with attention-deficit/hyperactivity disorder: Peer relationships and peer-oriented interventions. In D. W. Nangle & C. A. Erdley (Eds.), *The role of friendship in psychological adjustment: New directions for child and adolescent development* (pp. 51–77). San Francisco: Jossey-Bass.

MTA Cooperative Group. (1999a). A 14-month randomized clinical trial of treatment strategies for attention-deficit hyperactivity disorder (ADHD). *Archives of General Psychiatry, 56*, 1073–1086.

MTA Cooperative Group. (1999b). Moderators and mediators of treatment response for children with attention-deficit/hyperactivity disorder: The multimodal treatment study of children with attention-deficit/hyperactivity disorder. *Archives of General Psychiatry, 56*, 1088–1096.

MTA Cooperative Group. (2004). National Institute of Mental Health multimodal treatment study of ADHD follow-up: 24 month outcomes of treatment strategies for adult attention-deficit/hyperactivity disorder. *Pediatrics, 113*(4), 754–761.

Murphy, K. (2005). Psychosocial treatments for ADHD in teens and adults: A practice-friendly review. *Journal of Clinical Psychology, 61*(5), 607–619.

Nadeau, K. G. (2005). Career choices and workplace challenges for individuals with ADHD. *Journal of Clinical Psychology, 61*(5), 549–563.

Nanson, J. L., & Hiscock, M. (1990). Attention deficits in children exposed to alcohol prenatally. *Alcoholism: Clinical & Experimental Research, 14*(5), 656–661.

National Institute of Health. (2006). *Drug Information*. Retrieved December 8, 2006, from http://www.nlm.nih.gov/services/drug.html.

Newcorn, J. H., & Halperin, J. M. (2000). Attention-deficit disorders with hyperactivity and aggression. In T. E. Brown (Ed.), *Attention deficit disorders and comorbidities in children, adolescents, and adults* (pp. 171–208). Washington, DC: American Psychiatric Press, Inc.

Nigg, J. T. (2001). Is ADHD a disinhibitory disorder? *Psychological Bulletin, 127*(5), 571–598.

Osterreith, P. A. (1944). Le test de copie d'une figure complexe [Complex Figure Test]. *Archives de Psychologie, 30*, 206–256.

Owens, E. B., Hinshaw, S. P., Kraemer, H. C., Arnold, L. E., Abikoff, H. B., Cantwell, D. P., et al. (2003). Which treatment for whom for ADHD: Moderators of treatment response in the MTA. *Journal of Consulting and Clinical Psychology, 71*(3), 540–552.

Pelham, W. E. (1993). Pharmacotherapy for children with attention-deficit hyperactivity disorder. *School Psychology Review, 22*, 199–227.

Pelham, W. E., Aronoff, H. R., Midlam, J. K., Shapiro, C. J., Gnagy, E. M., Chronis, A. M., et al. (1999). A comparison of Ritalin and Adderall: Efficacy and time-course in children with attention-deficit/hyperactivity disorder. *Pediatrics, 103*, 43.

Pelham, W. E., Burrows-Maclean, L., Gnagy, E. M., Fabiano, G. A., Coles, E. K., Tesco, K. E., et al. (2005). Transdermal methylphenidate, behavioral, and combined treatment for children with ADHD. *Experimental and Clinical Psychopharmacology, 13*(2), 111–126.

Pelham, W. E., Fabiano, G. A., Gnagy, E. M., Greiner, A. R., Hoza, B., Manos, M., & Janakovic, F. (2005). Comprehensive psychosocial treatment for ADHD. In E. Hibbs & P. Jensen (Eds.), *Psychosocial treatments for child and adolescent disorders: Empirically based strategies for clinical practice* (2nd ed., pp. 377–410). New York: APA Press.

Pelham, W. E., & Washbusch, D. A. (1999). Behavioral interventions in attention-deficit/hyperactivity disorder. In H. Quay & A. Hogan (Eds.), *Handbook of disruptive behavior disorders* (pp. 255–278). New York: Kluwer Academic/Plenum.

Pfiffner, L. J., Calzada, E., & McBurnett, K. (2000). Interventions to enhance social competence. *Child and Adolescent Psychiatric Clinics of North America, 9*, 689–709.

Pfiffner, L. J., & McBurnett, K. (1997). Social skills training with parent generalization: Treatment effects for children with attention-deficit disorder. *Journal of Consulting and Clinical Psychology, 65*, 749–757.

Pisterman, S., McGrath, P., Firestone, P., Goodman, J. T., Webster, I., & Mallory, R. (1989). Outcome of parent-mediated treatment of preschoolers with attention deficit disorder with hyperactivity. *Journal of Consulting and Clinical Psychology, 57*(5), 628–635.

Pliszka, S. R., Borcherding, S. H., Spratley, K., Leon, S., & Irick, S. (1997). Measuring inhibitory control in children. *Journal of Developmental and Behavioral Pediatrics, 18*, 254–259.

Pomerleau, O., Downey, K., Stelson, F. & Pomerleau, C. (1995). Cigarette smoking in adult patients diagnosed with attention deficit hyperactivity disorder. *Journal of Substance Abuse, 7*, 373–378.

Quinlan, D. M. (2000). Assessment of attention-deficit/hyperactivity disorder and comorbidities. In T.E. Brown (Ed.), *Attention-deficit disorders and comorbidities in children, adolescents, and adults* (pp. 455–508). Washington, DC: American Psychiatric Press, Inc.

Ramsay, J. R., & Rostain, A. L. (2005). Adapting psychotherapy to meet the needs of adults with attention-deficit/hyperactivity disorder. *Psychotherapy: Theory, Research, Practice, Training, 42*(1), 72–84.

Rickel, A. U., & Becker-Lausen, E. (1997). *Keeping children from harm's way*. Washington, DC: American Psychological Assocoiation.

Riddle, M. A., Nelson, J. C., Kleinman, C. S., Rasmusson, A., Leckman, J. F., King, A., & Cohen, D. (1991). Sudden death in children receiving Norpramin: A review of three reported cases and commentary. *Journal of the American Academy of Child and Adolescent Psychiatry, 31*, 1062–1069.

Rieff, M. I., & Tippins, S. (2004). *ADHD: A complete and authoritative guide*. Oak Grove Village, IL: American Association of Pediatrics.

Rietveld, M. J., Hudziak, J. J., Bartels, M., van Beijsterveldt, C. E., & Boomsma, D. I. (2004). Heritability of attention problems in children: Longitudinal results from a study of twins, age 3 to 12. *Journal of Child Psychology and Psychiatry, 45*(3), 577–588.

Riggs, P. (1998). Clinical approach to treatment of ADHD in adolescents with substance use disorders and conduct disorder. *Journal of the American Academy of Child and Adolescent Psychiatry, 37*, 331–332.

Riggs, P. D., Thompson, L. L., & Mikulich, S. K., Whitmore, E. A., & Crowley, E. A. (1996). An open trial of pemoline in drug dependent delinquents with attention deficit hyperactivity disorder. *Journal of the American Academy of Child and Adolescent Psychiatry, 35*, 1018–1024.

Riordan, H. J., Flashman, L. A., Saykin, A. J., Frutiger, S. A., Carroll, K. E., & Huey, L. (1999). Neuropsychological correlates of methylphenidate treatment in adult ADHD with and without depression. *Archives of Clinical Neuropsychology, 14*, 217–233.

Robertson, M. M., & Eapen, V. (1992). Pharmocologic controversy of CNS stimulants in Gilles de la Tourette syndrome. *Clinical Neuropharmacology, 15*, 408–425.

Robin, A. L. (1998). *ADHD in adolescents: Diagnosis and treatment*. New York: Guilford Press.

Rohde, L. A., Szobot, C., Polanczyk, G., Schmitz, M., Martins, S., & Tramontina, S. (2005). Attention-deficit/hyperactivity disorder in a diverse culture: Do research and clinical findings support the notion of a cultural construct for the disorder? *Biological Psychiatry, 57*(11), 1436–1441.

Rugino, T. A., & Samsock, T. C. (2003). Modafinil in children with attention-deficit hyperactivity disorder. *Pediatric Neurology, 29*, 136–142.

Safer, D. J., Zito, J. M., & Gardner, J. F. (2001). Pemoline hepatotoxicity and postmarketing surveillance. *Journal of the American Academy of Child and Adolescent Psychiatry, 40*, 622–629.

Safren, S. A., Otto, M. W., Sprich, S., Winett, C. L., Wilens, T. E., & Biederman, J. (2005). Cognitive-behavioral therapy for ADHD in medication-treated adults with continued symptoms. *Behavioral Research and Therapy, 43*(7), 831–42.

Schachar, R. J., Tannock, R., Cunningham, C., & Corkum, P. V. (1997). Behavioral, situational and temporal effects of treatment of ADHD with methylphenidate. *Journal of the American Academy of Child and Adolescent Psychiatry, 36*, 754–763.

Semrud-Clikeman, M., Filpek, P. A., Biederman, J., Steingard, R., Kennedy, D., Renshaw, P., & Bekken, K. (1994). Attention-deficit hyperactivity disorder: Magnetic resonance imaging morphometric analysis of the corpus callosum. *Journal of the American Academy of Child and Adolescent Psychiatry, 39*, 477–484.

Semrud-Clikeman, M., Steingard, R., Filpek, P., Biederman, J., Bekken, K., & Renshaw, P. F. (2000). Using MRI to examine brain-behavior relationships in males with attention-deficit disorder with hyperactivity. *Journal of the American Academy of Child and Adolescent Psychiatry, 39*, 477–484.

Shepard, B. A., Carter, A. S., & Cohen, J. E. (2000). Attention-deficit/hyperactivity disorder and the preschool child. In T. E. Brown (Ed.), *Attention-deficit disorders and vomor-*

*bidities in children, adolescents, and adults* (pp. 407–436). Washington, DC: American Psychiatric Press, Inc.

Sherman, M., & Hertzig, M. E. (1991). Prescribing practices of Ritalin: The Suffolk County, New York study. In L. L. Greenhill & B. B. Osman (Eds.), *Ritalin: Theory and patient management* (pp. 187–193). New York: Mary Ann Liebert.

Silver, L. (1992). *Attention deficit hyperactivity disorder: A clinical guide to diagnosis and treatment.* Washington, DC: American Psychiatric Press.

Sinha, G. (2004). Training the brain: Cognitive therapy as an alternative to ADHD drugs. *Scientific American, 293*(1), 22–3.

Solhlkhah, R., Wilens, T. E., Daly, J., Prince, J. B., Van Patten, S. L., & Biederman, J. (2005). Buproprion SR for the treatment of substance-abusing outpatient adolescents with attention-deficit/hyperactivity disorder and mood disorders. *Journal of Child and Adolescent Psychopharmacology, 15*(5), 777–786.

Spencer, T. J. (2004). ADHD treatment across the life cycle. *Journal of Clinical Psychiatry, 65*(Suppl 3), 22–6.

Spencer, T., Wilens, T., Biederman, J., Faraone, S. V., Ablon, J. E., & Lapey, K. (1995). A double-blind, crossover comparison of methylphenidate and placebo in adults with childhood-onset attention-deficit hyperactivity disorder. *Archives of General Psychiatry, 52*, 434–443.

Spencer, T., Wilens, T., Biederman, J., Wozniak, J., & Harding-Crawford, M. (2000). Attention-deficit/hyperactivity disorder with mood disorders. In T. E. Brown (Ed.), *Attention-deficit disorders and comorbidities in children, adolescents, and adults* (pp. 79–124). Washington, DC: American Psychiatric Press, Inc.

Stiefel, I. (1997). Can disturbance in attachment contribute to attention deficit hyperactivity disorder? A case discussion. *Clinical Child Psychology & Psychiatry, 2*(1), 45–64.

Still, G. F. (1902). Some abnormal psychical conditions in children. *Lancet, I*, 1008–1012.

Stine, J. J. (1994). Psychosocial and psychodynamic issues affecting noncompliance with stimulant treatment. *Journal of Child and Adolescent Psychopharmocology, 4*, 75–86.

St. Sauver, J. L., Barbaresi, W. J., Katusic, S. K., Colligan, R. C., Weaver, A. L., & Jacobsen, S. J. (2004). Early life risk factors for attention-deficit/hyperactivity disorder: A population-based cohort study. *Mayo Clinic Proceedings, 79*(9), 1124–1131.

Tannock, R., & Brown, T. E. (2000). Attention-deficit disorders with learning disorders in children and adolescents. In T. E. Brown (Ed.), *Attention deficit disorders and comorbidities in children, adolescents, and adults* (pp. 231–296). Washington, DC: American Psychiatric Press, Inc.

Tannock, R., Schachar, R., & Logan, G. (1995). Methylphenidate and cognitive flexibility: Dissociated dose effects in hyperactive children. *Journal of Abnormal Child Psychology, 23*, 235–266.

Taylor, E. (1999). Developmental neuropsychopathology of attention deficit and impulsiveness. *Development and Psychopathology, 11*(3), 607–628.

Thapar, A., Fowler, T., Rice, F., Scourfield, J., van den Bree, M., Thomas, H., et al. (2003). Maternal smoking during pregnancy and attention deficit hyperactivity disorder symptoms in offspring. *American Journal of Psychiatry, 160*(11), 1985–1989.

Tully, L. A., Arseneault, L., Caspi, A., Moffitt, T. E., & Morgan, J. (2004). Does maternal warmth moderate the effects of birth weight on twins' attention deficit/hyperactivity disorder (ADHD) symptoms and low IQ? *Journal of Consulting and Clinical Psychology, 72*(2), 218–226.

Tutty, S., Gephart, H., & Wurzbacher, K. (2003). Enhancing behavioral and social skill functioning in children newly diagnosed with attention-deficit hyperactivity disorder in a pediatric setting. *Journal of Developmental and Behavioral Pediatrics, 24*, 51–57.

Turner, D. C., Clark, L., Dowson, J., Robbins, T. W., & Sahakian, B. J. (2004). Modafinil improves cognition and response inhibition in adult attention-deficit/hyperactivity disorder. *Biological Psychiatry, 55*(10), 1031–40.

Wechsler, D. (1997). *Wechsler Adult Intelligence Scale-III.* San Antonio, TX: Psychological Corporation.

Weiss, G., & Hechtman, L. (1986). *Hyperactive children grown up.* New York: Guilford.

Weiss, M., Hechtman, L. T., & Weiss, G. (1999). *ADHD in adulthood: a guide to current theory, diagnosis, and treatment.* Baltimore, MD: The Johns Hopkins University Press.

Wells, K. C., Pelham, W. E., Kotkin, R. A., Hoza, B., Abikoff, H. B., Abramowitz, A. et al. (2000). Psychosocial treatment strategies in the MTA study: Rationale, methods, and critical issues in design and implementation. *Journal of Abnormal Child Psychology, 28,* 483–505.

Whitaker, A. H., Van Rossem, R., Feldman, J. F., Schonfeld, I. S., Pinto-Martin, J. A., Tore, C., Shaffer, D., & Paneth, N. (1997). Psychiatric outcomes in low-birth-weight children at age 6 years: Relation to neonatal cranial ultrasound abnormalities. *Archives of General Psychiatry, 54*(9), 847–856.

Whitman, B. Y. (2000). Adult outcomes for persons with attention deficit/hyperactivity disorder. In P. J. Accardo, T. A. Blondis, B. Y. Whitman, & M. A. Stein (Eds.), *Attention deficits and hyperactivity in children and adults* (pp. 685–697). New York: Marcel Dekker, Inc.

Wilens, T. E., Biederman, J., Baldessarini, R. J., Geller, B., Schleifer, D., Spencer, T. J., et al. (1996). Cardiovascular effects of therapeutic doses of tricyclic antidepressants in children and adolescents. *Journal of the American Academy of Child and Adolescent Psychiatry, 35,* 1491–1501.

Wilens, T. E., Biederman, J., Prince, J., Spencer, T. J., Faraone, S. V., Warburton, R., et al. (1996). A double-blind, placebo-controlled trial for adults with ADHD. *American Journal of Psychiatry, 153,* 1147–1153.

Wilens, T. E., Faraone, S .V., Biederman, J., & Gunawardene, S. (2003). Does stimulant therapy of attention-deficit/hyperactivity disorder beget later substance abuse? A meta-analytic review of the literature. *Pediatrics, 111*(1), 179–85.

Wilens, T. E., McDermott, S. P., Biederman, J., Abrantes, A., Hakesy, A., & Spencer, T. J. (1999). Cognitive therapy in the treatment of adults with ADHD: A systematic chart review of 26 cases. *Journal of Cognitive Psychotherapy: An International Quarterly, 13,* 215–226.

Wilens, T. E., & Spencer, T. J. (2000). The stimulants revisited. *Child and Adolescent Psychiatry Clinics of North America, 9,* 573–603.

Wilens, T. E., Spencer, T. J., & Biederman, J. (2000a). Attention-deficit/hyperactivity disorder with substance abuse disorders. In T. E. Brown (Ed.), *Attention deficit disorders and comorbidities in children, adolescents, and adults* (pp. 319–339). Washington, DC: American Psychiatric Press, Inc.

Wilens, T. E., Spencer, T. J., & Biederman, J. (2000b). Pharmacotherapy of attention-deficit/hyperactivity disorder. In T. E. Brown (Ed.), *Attention-deficit disorders and comorbidities in children, adolescents, and adults* (pp. 509–536). Washington, DC: American Psychiatric Press, Inc.

Wolraich, M. L., Lindgren, S. D., Stumbo, P. J., Stegink, L. D., Appelbaum, M. I., & Kiritsy, M. C. (1994). Effects of diets high in sucrose or aspartame on the behavior and cognitive performance of children. *New England Journal of Medicine, 330,* 302–327.

World Health Organization. (1992). *The ICD-10 Classification of Mental and Behavioural Disorders.* Genenva, Author.

Zametkin, A. J., & Rapoport, J. L. (1986). The pathophysiology of attention deficit disorder with hyperactivity: A review. In B. B. Lahey & A. E. Kazdin (Eds.), *Advances in clinical child psychology,* (Vol. 9, pp. 177–216). New York: Plenum Press.

# Appendix: Tools and Resources

## Support Groups and Organizations for Individuals and Professionals

The Attention Deficit Information Network, Inc.
58 Prince St.
Needham, MA 02492
U.S.A.
Tel.: +1 781-455-9895
Web site: http://www.addinfonetwork.com
Support and information is offered to families of children with ADD, adults with ADD, and professionals through a network of AD-IN chapters.

ADD Warehouse
3200 Northwest 70th Ave., Suite 102
Plantation, FL 33317
U.S.A.
Tel.: +1 800-233-9273
Web site: http://addwarehouse.com
Is a central location for ordering books, tapes, assessment scales, and videos carefully selected to help parents, educators, and health professionals assist people affected by developmental disorders, including ADHD and related disorders.

Center for Mental Health Services
5600 Fishers Lane, Room 15-105
Rockville, MD 20857
U.S.A.
Tel.: +1 800-789-2647
Web site: http://www.samhsa.gov
A branch of the U.S. Department of Health and Human Services that provides a range of information on mental health, treatment, and support services.

Children and Adults with Attention Deficit Disorders (CHADD)
8181 Professional Place, Suite 150
Landover, MD 20785
U.S.A.
Tel.: +1 800-233-4050
Web site: http://www.chadd.org
This group advocates for those with ADHD. Website has "Frequently Asked Questions" section and offers information on legal rights.

Council for Exceptional Children
1110 North Glebe Road
Suite 300
Arlington, VA 22201-5704
U.S.A.
Tel.: +1 800-CEC-SPED (800-232-7733)
Web site: http://www.cec.sped.org
Supplies materials for educators to use in working with children.

ERIC Clearinghouse on Disabilities and Gifted Education
1110 North Glebe Road
Arlington, VA 22201-5704
U.S.A.
Tel.: +1 800-328-0272
Web site: http://www.ericec.org
ERIC (Educational Resources Information Center) is a part of the U.S. Department of Education. This organization provides information on the education of individuals with disabilities as well as those who are gifted.

Federation of Families for Children's Mental Health
1101 King St.
Alexandria, VA 22314
U.S.A.
Tel.: +1 703-684-7710
Web site: http://www.ffcmh.org
The Federation serves the needs of children with serious emotional, behavioral, and mental disorders and their families. Includes publications, information on related seminars and workshops, speaker's bureau, crisis intervention and support groups.

Health Resource Center
The George Washington University
2121 K St., NW, Suite 220
Washington, DC 20037
U.S.A.
Tel.: +1 800-544-3284
Web site: http://www.heath.gwu.edu
Provides information on financial aid for students with disabilities, including Federal aid, state vocational rehabilitation services, and regional and local sources.

National Center for Learning Disabilities
381 Park Ave., South Suite 1401
New York, NY 10016
U.S.A.
Tel.: +1 212-545-7510
Web site: http://www.ld.org
The Center offers information, resources, referral services, and advocates for more effective policies.

National Clearinghouse for Alcohol and Drug Information
PO Box 2345
Rockville, MD 20847
U.S.A.
Tel.: +1 800-729-6686
Web site: http://ncadi.samhsa.gov/
Information on the risks of alcohol use during pregnancy, and fetal alcohol syndrome is provided.

National Information Center for Children and Youth with Disabilities (NICHCY)
PO Box 1492
Washington, DC 20013
U.S.A.
Tel.: +1 800-695-0285
Web site: http://www.nichcy.org
Provides information about disabilities in children and youth. "Good Frequently Asked" questions site on web. Lists resources in every state, including Parent Training and Information Centers (PTI).

U.S. Department of Education Office of Special Education Programs
400 Maryland Ave., SW
Washington, DC 20202
U.S.A.
Tel.: +1 1-800-USA-LEARN (1-800-872-5327)
Web site: http://www.ed.gov/about/offices/list/osers/osep/index.html
Excellent site for information on Parent Training and Information Centers (PTI).

National Institute of Mental Health
Office of Communications
6001 Executive Boulevard, Room 8184, MSC 9663
Bethesda, Maryland, MD 20892-9663
U.S.A.
Tel.: +1 301-443-4513 or 1-866-615-NIMH (6464) toll-free
TTY: 301-433-8431
Fax: 301-443-4279
Fax 4U: 301-443-5158
E-mail: nimhinfo@nih.gov
Web site: http://www.nimh.nih.gov
A comprehensive resource for information on research into the brain, behavior, and mental disorders.

CLINICAL HANDBOOK OF
**Psychotropic Drugs**
for Children and Adolescents

KALYNA Z. BEZCHLIBNYK-BUTLER · ADIL S. VIRANI (EDS.)

second revised edition

HOGREFE

*Kalyna Z. Bezchlibnyk-Butler, Adil S. Virani* (Editors)

# Clinical Handbook of Psychotropic Drugs for Children and Adolescents

2nd, revised and expanded edition May 2007, ca. 360 pages
spiral-bound, ca, US $69.00 / € 59.95, ISBN: 978-0-88937-309-9

**A new edition of the highly acclaimed psychotropic drug reference for all clinicians dealing with children and adolescents!**

This book is designed to fill a need for a comprehensive but compact and easy-to-use reference for all mental health professionals dealing with children and adolescents. The new edition of the widely praised handbook summarizes the latest information from the published literature (scientific data, controlled clinical trials, case reports) and clinical experience in compact and easy-to-use charts and bulleted lists for each class of psychotropic drug used in children and adolescents.

The spiralbound handbook includes for each class of drugs both monograph statements on use in children and adolescents and approved indications, as well as the available data concerning off-label indications, findings from open and double-blind studies concerning doses, adverse effects, and other considerations in these age groups.

For each class of drug, summary information is provided on:

- Classification
- Product availability
- Indications
- Pharmacology
- Dosing
- Pharmacokinetics
- Adverse effects
- Withdrawal
- Precautions
- Toxicity
- Nursing implications
- Drug interactions
- Contraindications
- Patient instructions
- Interactions

**From the reviews of the first edition**

*"Authoritatively and exhaustively compiles currently available information in a user-friendly form...The aim of the Handbook is to be a source of 'fast facts' for the busy clinician...an aim it achieves splendidly."* M. Gittelman, *Int J Mental Health* 2005

*"Well-researched...An essential reference book...all professionals should have...Full of indispensable information and data in a sequenced and logical design."* P. Shelley, *Drogo Res – Int J Psychiatric Nursing Res*, 2004

*"Provides the busy clinician with all the information that is essential for those prescribing a psychotropic drug to a child or adolescent...Very 'user friendly'...Highly recommended to all clinicians that specialize in treating children and adolescents."* B.E. Leonard, in *Human Psychopharmacol*, 2005

*"If you see children who are placed on psychotropic medications, this books clearly falls into your 'must-have' category."* J.C. Courtney, in *Child Neuropsychol*, 2005

**Table of contents**

Order online at: **www.hhpub.com** or call toll-free **(800) 228-3749**
please quote "APT 2007" when ordering

HOGREFE

Hogrefe & Huber Publishers · 30 Amberwood Parkway · Ashland, OH 44805
Tel: (800) 228-3749 · Fax: (419) 281-6883
Hogrefe & Huber Publishers · Rohnsweg 25 · D-37085 Göttingen
Tel: +49 551 49 609-0 · Fax: +49 551 49 609-88
E-Mail: custserv@hogrefe.com

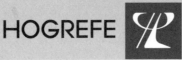

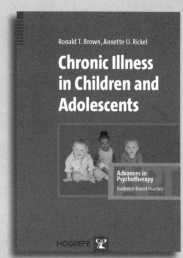
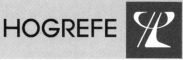

# Advances in Psychotherapy – Evidence-Based Practice

**Keep Up with the Advances in Psychotherapy!**

Developed and edited in consultation with the Society of Clinical Psychology (APA Division 12).

## Pricing / Standing Order Terms

Regular Prices: Single-volume – $24.95; Series Standing Order – $19.95
APA D12 member prices: Single-volume – $19.95; Series Standing Order – $17.95

With a Series Standing Order you will automatically be sent each new volume upon its release. After a minimum of 4 successive volumes, the Series Standing Order can be cancelled at any time. If you wish to pay by credit card, we will hold the details on file but your card will only be charged when a new volume actually ships.

**Order Form** (please check a box)

[ ] I would like to place a Standing Order for the series at the special price of US $ / €19.95 per volume, starting with volume no. ..........

[ ] I am a D12 Member and would like to place a Standing Order for the series at the special D12 Member Price of US $ / € 17.95 per volume, starting with volume no. ......
My APA membership no. is:

[ ] I would like to order the following single volumes at the regular price of US $ / € 24.95 per volume.

[ ] I am a D12 Member and would like to order the following single volumes at the special D12 Member Price of US $ / € 19.95 per volume.
My APA D12 membership no. is:

| Qty. | Author / Title / ISBN | Price | Total |
|------|------------------------|-------|-------|
|      |                        |       |       |
|      |                        |       |       |
|      |                        |       |       |
|      | Subtotal               |       |       |
|      | WA residents add 8.8% sales tax | | |
|      | Shipping & handling:<br>USA – US $6.00 per volume (multiple copies: US $1.25 for each further copy)<br>Canada – US $8.00 per volume (multiple copies: US $2.00 for each further copy)<br>South America: – US $10.00 per volume (multiple copies: US $2.00 for each further copy)<br>Europe: – € 6.00 per volume (multiple copies: € 1.25 for each further copy)<br>Rest of the World: – € 8.00 per volume (multiple copies: € 1.50 for each further copy) | | |
|      | Total                  |       |       |

[ ] Check enclosed [ ] Please bill me [ ] Charge my: [ ] VISA [ ] MC [ ] AmEx

Card # _____ CVV2/CVC2/CID # _____ Exp date _____

Signature _____

Shipping address (please include phone & fax) _____

_____
_____
_____
_____

Order online at: **www.hhpub.com** or call toll-free **(800) 228-3749**
please quote "APT 2007" when ordering

**HOGREFE**

Hogrefe & Huber Publishers · 30 Amberwood Parkway · Ashland, OH 44805
Tel: (800) 228-3749 · Fax: (419) 281-6883
Hogrefe & Huber Publishers · Rohnsweg 25 · D-37085 Göttingen
Tel: +49 551 49 609-0 · Fax: +49 551 49 609-88
E-Mail: custserv@hogrefe.com